D1289918

Sixties Fashion

Sixties Fashion
From Less is More to Youthquake

306 illustrations, 176 in color

Jonathan Walford

Thames & Hudson

For Chris

Page 2: One of six 'Union Jill' models attending
a British export promotion at the International
Motor Show in Geneva, March 1967.

Sixties Fashion © 2013 Jonathan Walford

Designed by This-Side

First published in 2013 in hardcover in the United States
of America by Thames & Hudson Inc., 500 Fifth Avenue,
New York, New York 10110

thamesandhudsonusa.com

Library of Congress Catalog Card Number 2012956325

ISBN 978-0-500-51693-5

Printed and bound in China by Toppan Leefung
Printing Co., Ltd

Contents

'The 1960s saw the death of fashion and the rise of style.'

For three centuries, women's fashions had been almost exclusively the invention of Parisian couturiers, but by 1962 the haute couture tradition was in jeopardy and Paris's domain over fashion was dwindling. New sources of style were on the rise from around the globe: London, New York, Florence, San Francisco, Hong Kong, Madrid, Rome...

Internationalism, originally a political movement that sought the input of many nations to work towards a common goal, became a model for modern fashion design. Architecture's interpretation of Internationalism resulted in a global style of Modernism, best illustrated by the glass-box office towers of North American cities. Internationalism in fashion meant that design was global. Eastern Bloc designers isolated from Western culture, such as Slava Zaistsev in the Soviet Union, Heinz Bormann in East Germany or Klara Rotschild in Hungary, used the same design principles as Pierre Cardin, Yves Saint Laurent and André Courrèges in Paris.

'Less is more' was the mantra of international Modernism. In fashion, this meant spare ornament and pure line, typical of the streamlined silhouettes of suits and shifts in the early 1960s. Ultimately, 'less is more' was best illustrated by the miniskirt, simply because less fabric showed more leg. It didn't mean plain and boring. The art scene was at a peak of creativity in the mid-1960s, as Minimalist and Abstract art styles were augmented by the Pop, Op and Psychedelic movements that found their way into fashion prints during the decade.

The world seemed to be living in a state of constant anxiety in the 1960s. However, despite a growing divorce rate, widening generation gap, soaring violent crime statistics, racial tension, wars, assassinations, riots and the threat of nuclear annihilation, there was optimism for the future, at least until the very end of the decade. This was evident in the excitement generated for the space program in the United States and the blockbuster attendance at World Expositions with hope-filled themes: Seattle's 'Space, Science and the Future' in 1962, New York's 'Peace Through Understanding' in 1964–65 and Montreal's 'Man and His World' in 1967. People believed in a future of world peace, lunar cities and one-piece jumpsuits that glowed in the dark and never needed ironing – polyester, paper, metal and mylar were the materials of the future.

The 1960s were all about change, largely caused by the shift in demographics that began with the first wave of post-war baby boom children coming of age early in the decade. As this generation grew in size, young people began to realize that they had the power to reinvent, rather than conform to, the world around them. This was especially evident in fashion. Young women wanted comfortable, affordable, informal but stylish clothes, not fitted, expensive, formal gowns. The rules of fashion started to break down. Diana Vreeland, editor-in-chief of US *Vogue*, saw the coming onslaught and called it a 'youthquake'.

London became the centre of a boutique revolution created by the young independent shopkeeper-designers who 'geared-up' their generation: the men in slim-cut suits and the women in girlish frocks. Many called themselves mods, short for Modernists, and London was at the heart of this scene. At the centre of the city a network of designers, musicians, models and photographers thrived on one another's energy. In a collective burst they created 'Swinging London' in the middle of the decade, captured in black and white by photographers Brian Duffy, David Bailey and Terence Donovan, and heard in the music of the Beatles, Rolling Stones and The Who. Fashions blossomed from the mod boutiques of London and followed the 'British invasion' of music as it swept across the US and around the world.

By the mid-1960s in the US, the younger generation was becoming restless. The hippie movement grew with the use of LSD and the escalation of American involvement in the war in Vietnam. True hippies believed in subversion through love and protest, and they made themselves identifiable by their anti-establishment and anti-materialistic appearance. They embraced the natural over the artificial and the plebeian over the elite; their individuality became a uniform of non-conformity.

The trend for protest and self-identity spread to black Americans who, in the midst of the Civil Rights movement, rediscovered and proclaimed their African heritage by wearing Moroccan dashikis and Afro hairstyles. The meaning of Internationalism was turned upside down at the end of the decade as the patterns and colours of different cultures were used to enrich mainstream fashion, which previously had relied on pure design. Tribalism in a globally connected world was a theme that would go on to flourish in future years, as would nostalgia. Fashion began referencing historical styles in the late 1960s as vintage clothing progressed from boutique novelty to prestigious fashion commodity, much as the past would become a dominant inspiration in later decades.

It could be said that the 1960s saw the death of fashion and the rise of style. By 1970, everything had changed from the way things had been just ten years before – the styles, markets, materials, demographics, inspirations and definitions of fashion were all new. 'Take it from me,' said designer Betsey Johnson in an interview with *New York* magazine in spring 2003. 'There will never be another chunk of time of such pure genius, from the invention of pantyhose to landing on the moon…. And it was the first and last time that fashion really, really changed.'

FOUNDATIONS: HIGH FASHION IN THE EARLY 1960s

1

'American women spent 1961 aping everything she wore, from her hair to her under-fitted suits and pillbox hats – the understated "Jackie look" was in.'

The first hint of what 1960s fashions would look like emerged in 1957, when the streamlined 'rocket ship' silhouette was introduced in the form of the sack dress. The shapeless sack made its wearers look like sleeved almonds, but the negated figure brought attention to the extremities of the body: the head and legs, the featured appendages of the 1960s. Women's hair began to take on the bouffant in 1957 – inflated, airy hairstyles brushed full and tossed like a salad atop the head, drawing the eye upwards from the figureless dress. At the other end, legs appeared longer and slimmer in towering stiletto-heeled shoes that made calves shapelier in hemlines hovering just below the knee.

Most clothes were a little more fitted in 1958, although at Dior, head designer Yves Saint Laurent's 'Trapeze' collection of tent-shaped dresses and coats for spring, and high waists for autumn, did not abandon an aerodynamic silhouette that anticipated the path fashion would take in the coming decade. Saint Laurent was looking for new ways to define the female form by shifting emphasis away from the exaggerated hourglass figure that Christian Dior himself had established as the ideal silhouette in 1947.

Coco Chanel had also set a standard by 1958 with her casually tailored suits with open jackets, contoured in tweed, hinting at the feminine form without relying upon the figure to give the suit its shape; older women looked more youthful and younger women more sophisticated in Chanel. By 1960 the Chanel suit was a mainstay of fashion and had been copied for every budget, in tweed for daytime and satin for cocktails.

Although Paris still dominated high fashion in 1960, competition was building. Norman Norell and James Galanos, for example, were respected as leaders of American dress design. However, many American women still thought there was something just a little extra-special about a Paris-designed dress or suit. *Life* reported on 14 March 1960 on the business of Ohrbach's, a New York clothier, copying Paris originals:

Above: Grey-and-pink tweed suit by CHANEL as pictured in US *Vogue*, 15 October 1961.

Page 8: Jacqueline Kennedy at her Georgetown home, August 1960.

Right: A copy of a CHANEL suit by New York manufacturer DAVIDOW using a different grey tweed but the same trim. DAVIDOW was known for its copies of CHANEL that often included the same fabrics and findings as the originals.

Above left: Beaded cocktail dress, made in Hong Kong, sold and worn in Montreal, *c.* 1964.

Above right: Blue silk dress by MARC BOHAN for CHRISTIAN DIOR, Paris, autumn 1962.

Left: Green silk quilted cocktail coat and ivory damask silk dress by DYNASTY, Hong Kong, early 1960s.

'Ohrbach's does [a] fast job making new Paris copies.... The clothes being so frantically unpacked were first shown at the Paris collections last month. This week they will be available to US customers in defy-the-eye copies at one tenth of their original cost.... [Ohrbach's] is the biggest line-for-line copyist of Paris clothes.... This season, expecting its biggest sales, Ohrbach's broke all its previous records by copying fifty Paris outfits.... Sometimes Ohrbach's sells nearly a thousand copies of a single outfit and the copies often rub elbows at social gatherings with the Paris originals. One reason for this popularity with high-style ladies as well as those on a budget is that Ohrbach's buys with an eye on what will copy well.... If the fabric cannot be duplicated here it may use the original and will often use original buttons and braid.'

As the decade progressed, Paris would lose its status as the sole delineator of high fashion. Italy had grown into a formidable player, and London was about to burst forth with fashions for the young. Fashion became an international aspiration for nations seeking the Western model of Modernism. Although the Far East had been a source of textiles and style inspiration for centuries, Asia was now becoming a part of the modern world, adopting new design and manufacturing methods while simultaneously infusing modern fashion.

It started in Hong Kong. Shanghai had originally been the centre of the Chinese fashion industry, but after the establishment of the People's Republic in 1949, most of that city's tailors, seamstresses and embroiderers migrated to Taiwan or the British colony of Hong Kong. By 1960 there were over a thousand tailors working in the island's Causeway Bay and Wan Chai districts, making custom suits and shirts for denizens, British representatives and visitors to the city.

A form-fitting dress that blended Western and Chinese styling called *cheungsam* (Cantonese for 'long shirt'), or *qi-pao* (Mandarin for Manchu 'banner robe') had developed for modern Chinese women in the 1920s and 1930s. Beautifully hand-finished and embroidered silk *cheungsams* as well as

silk pyjama sets were popular Hong Kong exports in the early 1950s. Recognizing a potential market for finely finished silk garments at affordable prices, New York manufacturer Bud Berman established the Dynasty label in 1953. Dynasty's stylist Dora Sanders merged high-fashion ideas with the *cheungsam*, adjusted proportions for the ideal hourglass-shaped Western figure, and created a variety of cocktail and evening-gown styles as well as late day suits. Top-end American retailers Neiman Marcus, I. Magnin and Lord & Taylor acquired exclusive rights to the new designs for six months before they were available through other retailers in the US and abroad, including in Hong Kong.

The *New York Times* reported on 8 September 1959 that 'clothes with the Dynasty label are sold in 595 stores throughout the United States...and on military bases all over the world.... Dynasty has become the leading fashion exporter in Asia.' Everything except the seaming was handmade in a Kowloon factory that employed 2,500 workers. 'More than 300 men control the orchestra of sewing machines. The women excel at hand-sewing and embroidery...the "frog girl"...sits for eight hours a day, skillfully looping, folding, and stitching tiny, brilliantly colored frog closings. She is paid by the piece – her average is forty a day.' This was the first time an American fashion house had manufactured its clothes in Hong Kong, and the results were highly profitable.

Dynasty was peaking in popularity in 1960 when *The World of Suzie Wong* was released. This film depicted Hong Kong as a romantic locale and fuelled interest in the Chinese-style fashions worn by its beautiful leading actress, Nancy Kwan. Around the same time, other manufacturers, such as New York-based Victoria Royal Ltd, set up business to compete with Dynasty. Hong Kong companies also manufactured for foreign markets, but companies not headquartered in the importing nation were hindered by quota limits. Nathan and Strong, a New York clothing company, imported hand-knitted and bead-embroidered evening dresses from a Hong Kong-based manufacturer that retailed for $400 in 1961. By 1964 the beaded dresses were being drolly referred to as 'floor-length tiaras' in New York fashion columns; Robert Strong, the founder of Nathan and Strong, said in an interview with the *New York Times* on 22 July 1964 that the garments reflected value that was impossible to duplicate in New York at three times the cost: 'They caught on so well that we can't get enough of them.'

Paris's largest export market in the early 1960s was the United States, and many French designers created fashions that would appeal to an American audience. Some had contracts to develop lines specifically for that country. The most successful of these was Christian Dior, who began a special relationship with the US in 1948. At first the line was created and made in France, but by 1961 the entire operation had been transplanted to New York, along with Guy Douvier, the Dior-appointed designer of the range, who would monitor the pulse of American fashion and reflect its tastes and direction in all his designs for the Dior New York label.

However, America was leading in the junior and sportswear markets, and its style press was reporting more about the domestic collections of both native-born and naturalized designers. The US had gained the confidence of its own citizenry and was now exporting its fashions to the world: Jonathan Logan dresses were sold in Germany, Sue Brett and Smartee lines were available in France, and the Majestic brand could be bought off the rack in the UK.

Stylistically, Paris and New York were in tune in 1960, especially when it came to hemlines. No longer would the length of dresses be measured by their relative distance from the floor, as had been the case since the first hem had showed a hint of ankle fifty years earlier. Hemlines were now being measured in relation to the knee, and for spring 1960 the consensus was two inches below.

With a redefined waist, full- and narrow-skirted dresses were equally popular for spring 1960, but there was a preference for a slimmer evening profile. The most popular evening fashion was a simple slip-cut dress, covered in white, silver or gold beads and sequins; jewel-tone beads and sequins were substituted for autumn. These glittering gowns, the majority manufactured in Hong Kong, made all other evening jewelry unnecessary, with perhaps the exception of a pair of earrings. For daytime, jewelry was used sparingly, consisting mostly of long gold chains and button earrings, or one striking brooch.

Paris and New York daytime fashions showcased sleeveless and collarless dresses for spring, many with bloused waists or draped cowl backs that brought attention to long necks and slim arms. When sleeves were present they were wider and shorter, sometimes even open in a kimono style. Norman Norell first showed full-skirted culottes in New York, but both Paris and New York liked full skirts for summer, and if they were not full, they were pleated or cut on the bias to allow for swingy, fluid movement.

Summer fashion colours for dresses and sportswear were bright and often printed in bold patterns. Abstract and Expressionist art inspired many printed silks with strong brush strokes and oversized floral designs – a trend that would continue for several years. Historical patterns also gained popularity: Liberty of London revived some of their early designs, and Renaissance-patterned metallic brocades and cut velvets appeared in cocktail and evening clothes.

While dresses were often bright, the colour palette for suits and coats was usually muted: all shades of brown from camel to chocolate, grey, loden green, black and gold; and a range of purples were added for autumn, especially for tweedy clothes (Chanel's use of tweed was epidemic). Exotic leather accessories also came to the fore, including lizard, alligator and crocodile in natural brown shades as well as dyed white or gold. Yves Saint Laurent used black crocodile for his beat-inspired autumn 1960 collection – his last before leaving the House of Dior.

For autumn 1960, most silhouettes were heavily influenced by the 1920s. In Paris, cloches topped sheath-style dresses

MEET MR. MORT

Above: Advertisement for culottes with sleeveless top by MR. MORT, New York, spring 1960.

Left: Red-print silk culottes by NORMAN NORELL, New York, spring 1960.

ADELE SIMPSON

Above: Advertisement for suit
with kimono-sleeved jacket
by ADELE SIMPSON, New York,
spring 1960.

Right: American orange, beige
and cocoa silk shantung dress
with coat, unlabelled, *c.* 1960.
Dresses were frequently offered
with matching jackets or coats,
or with linings matching the dress,
in 1960. Shortened by an inch, this
set was worn by the original owner
on 22 November 1963 when she
shook President Kennedy's hand
as he left the Texas Hotel in Forth
Worth on his way to Dallas, where
he would be assassinated.

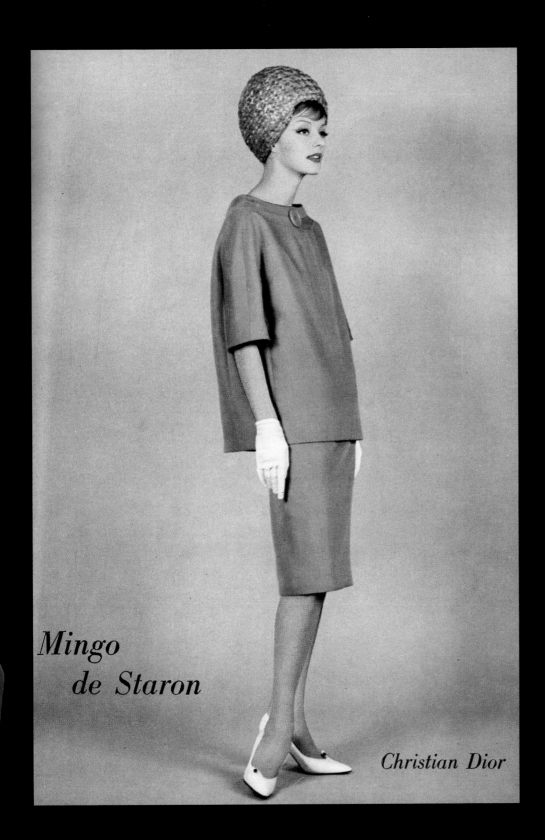

*Mingo
de Staron*

Christian Dior

Aléoutienne
imprimée

Lanvin Castillo

with de-emphasized waists. In New York, Norman Norell also showed cloche hats on models with debutante slouches – the fashionable pose of the 1920s created by rounding the shoulders forward while leaning backwards. His sequined silk jersey 'Mermaid' gowns for evening were worn by models done up like vamps from the silent film era, complete with shingled hair, pale face-powder and kohl-rimmed eyes. His collarless columnar coats that hung from the shoulders echoed the 1920s, but in oversized tweeds, plaids and checks.

In late 1960, thirty-one-year-old Jacqueline Kennedy became the leading American fashion icon. She possessed a model's figure and carried herself with elegant poise. Some criticized her hatless, bouffant hair and Parisian clothes, so she tamed her hairstyles enough to wear hats on more occasions, winning the approval of more conservative women, as well as the American hat industry. To quell rumours of her penchant for French couture, Mrs Kennedy commissioned American designer Oleg Cassini to create her inaugural day suit of sable-trimmed fawn wool, and asked Ethel Frankau of elite New York clothier Bergdorf Goodman's custom salon to make her inaugural ballgown of off-white chiffon and faille. American women spent the first half of 1961 aping everything

Opposite left: Artistic brush-print dress in black and brown on white silk by ELIANE MONTIGNY, Paris, c. 1960–61.

Opposite right: Bold print dress by LANVIN CASTILLO, Paris, spring 1960.

Right: Brown wool two-piece dress by BALENCIAGA, Paris, autumn 1961.

Far right: PIERRE CARDIN's take on the 1920s, Paris, spring 1961.

she wore, from her hair and full eyebrows to her under-fitted suits and pillbox hats – the understated 'Jackie look' was in. *Life* even reported in its 20 January 1961 issue of fashion mannequins being made in her likeness.

For spring 1961, the 1920s continued as a dominant inspiration for fashion. Top designers embraced unfitted clothes: collars disappeared from dresses to accentuate the length of the neck while hats grew taller and wider to elongate the figure. Designers from Rome to New York loved the return of the flapper and most showed unwaisted dresses, some with pleated skirts, and clutch coats. Pink was popular for spring and summer, but how to accessorize with colour was a personal choice – a woman could use several tones of the same shade in one outfit, or match some accessories exactly in colour, featuring the coat or hat in an entirely different shade. The most skilled successfully combined different coloured accessories in one outfit.

Sportswear was becoming considerably more informal, taking inspiration from the American fondness for blue jeans. *Life* featured hipster trousers in its 25 August 1961 issue: 'Inspired by American cowboy's jeans, in St Tropez, Mme Vachon designs them quite tight with tapered legs and worn with bare midriff bolero tops. In England, they are worn with bell bottoms and tailored blouses as shown by Mary Quant for fall.' In return, women in the US finally began to wear French bikinis. Buxom European beauties such as Brigitte Bardot and Ursula Andress had made them famous at Cannes and St Tropez for years, but the only place to see a belly-button-baring bikini in the US was a girlie magazine. It was only after the overtly wholesome Sandra Dee sported a modest bikini in the 1959 film *Gidget* that they slowly began to be bought, mostly for private poolside use; one-piece swimsuits still dominated at public beaches. The prudish resistance to wearing bikinis in the US became fodder for a song in the summer of 1960 by teen singer Brian Hyland, who had a number one hit with 'Itsy Bitsy Teenie Weenie Yellow Polka Dot Bikini'.

Back in Paris, in 1961 French couture was experiencing economic difficulties. As part of the reconstruction of the couture industry in 1952, the textile industry had been taxed, with the proceeds being used to subsidize the costs of producing model pieces for haute couture collections. The couture houses were required to use French textiles for 90 per cent of their fashions in order to be eligible to receive a portion of the subsidy, which was paid out according to the revenue earned in overseas trade. Dior was the recipient of the lion's share of the subsidy, which totalled about US $750,000 per year (the equivalent of more than $3 million today). With the loss of this government subsidy, most fashion houses dropped the number of models shown in their collections (spring 1962 shows were about one third smaller than usual). No longer tied to using French textiles, couturiers now looked to other sources – predominantly Switzerland and Germany, but also Thailand for slubby shantung silks and cotton sarongs, Burma and Japan for brocades, and India for gilt-thread-embroidered saris. The jet age had shrunk the world and made goods from the Far East more affordable and easier to obtain. The result was a decidedly exotic flair in many collections.

By the autumn of 1961 it was apparent that the simple fashions popular with Jacqueline Kennedy were not for every American woman. Many collections featured a return to figure-flattering styles with longer jackets and skirts flared or widened below the hip, gored or darted to give freedom of motion. For day, coat dresses, occasionally in a princess line, and other sheath styles appeared. With the emphasis returning to the feminine silhouette, colours dimmed to foggy greys, browns and black – especially black matelassé or velvet for evening. *Breakfast at Tiffany's* was the year's most fashion-influential film and made Audrey Hepburn an international icon: wide-brimmed hats, large sunglasses and sleeveless black dresses were in. Jacqueline Kennedy and Audrey Hepburn were both influential when it came to footwear as sharp, pointed-toe stiletto-heeled pumps lost ground to lower-heeled pumps with oval or square toes.

Above and right: Indian gilt-thread-embroidered black silk après-ski top by CHARLES DUMAS, Switzerland, c. 1961, and a photograph of a model wearing a similar top in the same fabric by JACQUES MARAUT, Paris, December 1961.

Life revelled at the perils of fashion footwear in a 10 October 1960 article that regaled the reader with the problems of spike heels and escalator foot treads, sticky road tar, grates and sewer covers. Five months later, on 24 March 1961, *Life* was pushing for smart and sensible styles in another shoe feature: 'The new thick heels are often in contrasting colors. This keeps them from being too "sensible" – a constant danger because the new heels are rarely more than two inches high…. Pointed toes, which…have been in style since 1957, are now being challenged by rounder toes, which conform more to the natural shape of the foot…. Square toes, introduced two years ago by Roger Vivier, shoe designer at the House of Dior, are catching on in less expensive versions. His newest "platypus" shoes – so called not for the animal's feet, but for its square snout – are two inches across. From Italy come the easiest of all to wear, open sandals. These have not been seen on US streets since the 1940s, but newly comfort-conscious women are apt to take to them for summer.'

Shot in 1959, the fashions of *La Dolce Vita* were not cutting edge by the time of the film's American release in April 1961, but the Italian styling was intoxicatingly glamorous – what could be chicer than sunglasses at night to avoid the glare of the paparazzi? Aristocratic Romans and the Vatican may not have approved of director Federico Fellini's morality, but despite the dissolute characters, the film underscored how influential Italy had become on the international fashion scene.

The Italian fashion industry had been reinvented during the country's post-war reconstruction. Italy had a seemingly

Right: Brown silk princess-line coat dress by TEAL TRAINA, New York, autumn 1961.

Middle: Green bouclé wool suit with longer, shaped jacket by GIVENCHY, Paris, autumn 1961.

Far right: White linen suit by FABIANI, Rome, *c*. 1961.

Right: CHARLES JOURDAN advertisement, March 1963.

Far right: Square-toe pump designed by ROGER VIVIER for CHRISTIAN DIOR, Paris, 1961.

Below: Various black leather mid-height heeled pumps by ONDINE, France, c. 1961–64.

inexhaustible pool of trained hand labourers who could produce beautifully finished *alla moda* fashions and footwear with lower labour costs than France. This combination created a successful industry, which contributed to the economic rebirth of the country, known as the 'Italian miracle', and a second Renaissance of Italian arts and industry. The label 'Made in Italy' was equated with contemporary chic as Italian style became the new way of being modern.

Life reported in a December 1961 feature article: 'In 1951 the first Italian fashion collections were…attended by only five buyers. Today the showings are held in Florence's magnificent Pitti Palace and are as devotedly attended as the Paris openings. Italy now exports more wearing apparel than any other country in the world. But Italy's fantastic fashion record does not rest on volume alone. Her designers have contributed an outstanding list of style changes. The new vogue [is] for knits…stretch pants for other than skiwear, scarf-print shirts, the pointed toe – even men's silk suits.'

The year 1962 was a pivotal one for Italian fashion: Roberto Capucci and Patrick de Barentzen both showed collections in Paris for the first time, while Simonetta and Fabiani, who had maintained rival ateliers in Rome since their marriage in 1953, joined forces and moved to Paris. Emilio Pucci also began designing couture from his Florence shop in 1962, elevating his name into high-fashion magazines. Pucci had become famous during the 1950s for his scarf print tops in bold patterns and striking colour combinations. His early career was largely built on sportswear made for export to American department stores or his boutiques in Florence and Rome. Pucci's print silk clothes were usually made up in classic styles that didn't date quickly: shirtwaists, tunics, Capri pants and blouses. His most popular garments with the jet set were in his soft, opaque-printed silk jersey that was ideal for travelling because it didn't wrinkle, never sagged and was as light as a feather. However, the silk jersey dresses were not lined, showed straps and garters, and were not forgiving of lumpy

figures. The fabric was also notorious for colour bleeds if it got wet, but the busy patterns successfully disguised small spots and stains. Pucci expanded his business in the early 1960s, opening boutiques in Paris, Gstaad in Switzerland and Portofino on the Italian Riviera. His clothes were in demand, even if they were relatively expensive: around US $100 for a dress in 1962 (approximately $750 today).

For the spring collections, Paris featured sketchy, bold prints – checks, dots, zebra stripes, and flowers in black and white with hand-drawn artsy effects. The season also saw the return of Yves Saint Laurent, now presenting under his own name. He included suits that had what he called a 'cowboy look', and evening clothes that evoked the silhouette of a rajah from an Eastern potentate. Perhaps his most influential style was a double-breasted gold-buttoned coat based on the pea coat that had been worn by the British navy for half a century. Along with Saint Laurent, Roberto Capucci, Patrick de Barentzen, André Courrèges (Balenciaga's former assistant) and Philippe Venet (Givenchy's former tailor) also debuted collections for spring 1962 in Paris.

In the US, the French-born designers Jacques Tiffeau, under his label Tiffeau & Busch, and Pauline Trigère were both winning fashion headlines in New York. Tiffeau was pushing for high-waisted silhouettes, while Trigère catered to a clientele who returned every year for the elegant capes, reversible coats, tailored suits and understated day dresses for which she was famous. Trigère had shown Eastern glamour in her rajah-influenced autumn 1961 collection, the season before Yves Saint Laurent, and continued to show rajah-style coats for day in spring 1962, while Saint Laurent's were for evening.

Alongside the nod to India, spring saw another exotic influence: the Cleopatra look. It was mostly noticeable in hair, make-up and jewelry, but manufacturers also used novelty Egyptian prints for everything from bathing suits to umbrellas, and high-end designers interpreted Cleopatra in evening clothes, using pleated and flowing fabrics in classical styles

Above: American advertisement for Italian scarf-print dresses and blouses, 1960.

Right: 'Roman Roads' print silk dress by PUCCI, Florence, c. 1960.

Pierre CARDIN

Robert BURG

Piqué de coton imprimé
de Robert Burg.
Production de Luigi · Milan

Left: Polka-dot dress by PIERRE
CARDIN, Paris, spring 1962.
The fabric was supplied by
textile magnate Robert Burg.

Above: Modernist-print linen tabard by CALIFORNIA GIRL, spring 1962.

Right: Dress by OLEG CASSINI using the same material, New York, 1962.

that clung to the figure. The inspiration came from the mounting anticipation of the upcoming film starring Elizabeth Taylor. The movie was plagued by problems and rife with gossip. By spring 1962 it had been in production for over two years and was already the most expensive film ever made. By summer the 'Cleo' fad was fading, a full year before the film finally debuted.

The fashion exoticism that was breaking ground in 1962 could also be found in the industry's choice of models. The fixation with northern European knockouts like Brigitte Bardot and Ann-Margaret was becoming inclusive of olive-skinned sirens like Gina Lollobrigida and Sophia Loren, as well as Asian beauties such as Hiroko Matsumoto, whom Pierre Cardin had brought to Paris from Japan to model his clothes in 1960, and Nancy Kwan, the British-Chinese star of the 1960 film *The World of Suzie Wong.* Christian Dior had been the first Paris fashion house to hire

black model Dorothea Towles in 1949. Aware of better opportunities in Paris, Ophelia DeVore, president of New York's Grace Del Marco Model Agency (a black-only agency), sent Helen Williams and La Jeune Hundley to Paris in 1960 where they were hired to model at Christian Dior and Jean Dessès, but in the US the two models were restricted to working only fashion shows for black audiences. Pauline Trigère broke the stigma of using black models when she hired twenty-three-year-old Beverly Valdes. According to a *New York Times* article from 23 June 1961, Trigère said, 'We only lost one customer in Birmingham, Alabama. We didn't miss her.' In the summer of 1962, Valdes was no longer alone on Seventh Avenue – Tiffeau & Busch and Arnold Scaasi had also hired black models for their shows.

For autumn 1962 designers were showing uncluttered shirtwaists, princess-line day dresses and tailored, fitted suits

with slim-cut sleeves. Rajah coats were now available for day and evening from many designers, accompanied by turbans to underscore the Indian styling. Without a turban, evening coiffures were intricately sculpted and lacquered into elaborate shapes, offsetting the column-thin evening dresses in flat wools, cut velvets or brocades.

Furs were everywhere: snow leopard, Indian lamb (white broadtail), fox, llama, mink, chinchilla and sable bound the collars and cuffs of coats and suits, or appeared as Cossack-sized hats for winter. *Life* reported on 2 November 1962: 'The more luxurious the fur, the more humble the styling. Trench coats are made up of the most precious pelts and have belts designed to be pulled in like the sash on a bathrobe. These poor-little-rich furs are played down to suit the taste of well-dressed women who for several winters have bypassed furs

in favour of simply cut cloth coats introduced by Balenciaga and Givenchy.' For those who could not afford fur, cloth trench coats remained popular and were shown paired with boots in fashion magazines and on runways, but despite the recommendation by fashion editors, boots were seldom worn in this way.

A slim, understated, minimalist look carried forward into 1963. Shoes were plain, jewelry was barely discernable and make-up was pale but for strongly emphasized eyes. Suits in textured wools and pale tweeds were precisely tailored, and cotton and linen were back in fashion. Paris showed white cotton matelassé evening gowns and linen organza blouses, and printed linen dresses and coats with coloured backgrounds. Bill Cunningham reported in *Women's Wear Daily* on 10 May 1963 what New York's socialites were wearing on the street: 'Here is the code: pastel suit – unbuttoned – chain-handled tiny

Black-and-white cotton matelassé evening dress with reverse-print coat by ARNOLD SCAASI, New York, c. 1963–65.

alligator bag – gold bracelets – natural colored gloves – two strand necklaces – no hat – low heeled shoes and no fur after March 1. If you don't stick to this code, you're definitely O U T.'

Marc Bohan made news at Dior with women's suits in men's chalk-striped wools. Coco Chanel carried on with her classic suits but in new fabrics: silk-and-wool ribbed blends with starched organza or silk cuffs and camisole. Givenchy's hit for the spring were little sleeveless linen dresses, some belted with narrow leather cords. Yves Saint Laurent's iconic dress from his spring 1963 collection was a navy wool shirt dress in nubby navy bouclé accented by a wide collar of white organdy. This simple dress appeared in every major spring fashion publication.

Menswear also offered inspiration for women's fashions in the US. Shirtwaist dresses and coats used men's cuffs and shirt collars, and some suits used men's shirt patterns for the jackets. Norman Norell borrowed the waistcoat and the V-neck sweater vest from sportswear to create three-piece day and evening outfits. Bill Blass, working for Maurice Rentner, followed Norell's lead for summer with vests under short-sleeved tailored linen suits. Running alongside masculine-inspired styles was a revival of an ultra-feminine empire dress silhouette shown by Oleg Cassini and Gustave Tassell. Both empire and shirt dress styles looked great in crêpe, a material that had seen little use since the 1940s. Both also took well to the Parisian penchant for white over the little black dress.

For evening, simple slim silhouettes were popular, including empire dresses made up in stark white crêpe, or black-and-white matelassé, or alternatively opulent fabrics such as jewel-toned velveteen or shimmering Indian brocade. Evening clothes were worn either with little cropped jackets or floor-length coats in the same fabric. The only jewelry needed was a pair of oversized earrings.

'At-home' clothes were becoming a distinct way of life and American designers led the way in creating informal but elegant full-length shifts and long skirts in bold colours and novel prints. One such print for summer 1963 was reptile.

Arnold Scaasi had started the fad when he used real snakeskin to make at-home pants for $1,000, but a fake snake print on cotton or silk felt better on the body and women's budgets. Fake fur brought a sense of humour to fashion, being used to imitate exotic pelts for unexpected garments such as ocelot slacks, leopard bathing suits and polar bear parkas. Improvements to vinyl now made it a better leather substitute, resulting in vinyl coats and skirts for autumn. And adding to a light touch of casual elegance in younger fashions, White Stag offered sweaters, skirts and ponchos in bold Picasso prints, bringing art to everyday dress – a trend that would grow stronger in 1964.

Autumn fashion continued the move towards a tailored easy style. Courrèges's small collection of very tailored suits and coats, all in white, from hats to boots, featured perfectly constructed welt seams. Most designer suits in Paris and elsewhere had slightly fitted or straight-hanging jackets, often shown over a man-tailored shirt, sometimes with a corduroy vest for a layered look, or two sweaters – a bulky mohair worn over a lightweight turtleneck. Under the skirt, a pair of cable-knit stockings and polished leather low-heeled ghillies or calf-high suede boots looked smart. Layers were ideal for warmth and the contrasts in textures and colours played against one another for some fashion excitement. For outerwear, trench coats in traditional poplin, and also suede, velveteen and fur were popular. *Life* reported on 30 August 1963: 'To the relief of women everywhere, the fall collections from Paris do not lower or raise hemlines, or ban or inflate the bosom. Instead of re-delineating the female anatomy, they crystallize and dramatize the new feeling for casual living that has swept the whole world.'

By the end of 1963, fashion was smart-looking and had lost much of the formal dressiness of the 1950s. The new look favoured a youthful elegance featuring tailored, tweedy styles for dressy daytime, a sporty relaxed chic for everyday and influences of the exotic for evening. Fashion was becoming younger and more international in scope.

YOUTHQUAKE:
FASHION BY
THE YOUNG
FOR THE YOUNG

'Couture is dead.
I want to design for the street.'

Emmanuelle Khanh, *Life*, 13 March 1964

In the mid-1930s a new category of women's fashions, termed 'junior', started being made by manufacturers around St Louis, Missouri, based upon market research carried out in the area. Junior fashions were designed to suit the leaner and less curvaceous youthful figure, appealing to the sportier tastes of younger women who didn't want to dress like their mothers. Recognizing that young women probably knew best what their own generation wanted, companies hired graduates from the fashion arts programme of Washington University in St Louis to create most of their junior collections. Department stores soon began carrying these lines in special sections designed to attract teens and college-age women; in New York, Bergdorf Goodman debuted its Miss Bergdorf department in August 1955 with a selection of junior and petite-sized clothes and accessories.

At the same time that the American ready-to-wear industry was tapping the youth market, there was a rise in youth-centric subcultures. In the US the clean-cut collegiate 'Ivy League' look, named after the Eastern Seaboard universities with football teams, rose in popularity during the 1950s and early 1960s. Young male Ivy Leaguers were particular about the brands and styles they wore, which included Bermuda shorts, Brooks Brothers suits, three-button coats and loafers. Their girlfriends wore cashmere sweaters and pleated tartan skirts. This clean-cut image was the antithesis of the motorcycle-riding greaser in black leather jacket, T-shirt and jeans. Then there was the anti-consumerist bohemian subculture known as the beat generation, who expressed themselves through free jazz and verse, existentialist literature and scruffy anti-fashion, including facial hair for men, heavy eyeliner for women, and sandals and black clothing for everyone.

By 1960 beat culture had spread from San Francisco and New York to Paris and then to London, where the Teddy boy movement had been around for a decade. Teddy boys were working-class young Englishmen who wore Edwardian-style long jackets with velvet collars and crêpe-soled shoes called brothel creepers. Teddy boys were avid fans of American rock 'n' roll, but by the early 1960s, rockers, who modelled their look after the jeans and leather jacket-clad American greaser, were displacing the older-style rock 'n' roll Teddy boys.

Following the American Motown and soul music scene, modernists, better known as mods, were Britain's newest youth movement in the early 1960s. The mod generation tended to be middle class and well educated, having benefited from post-war education subsidies along with an unprecedented growth in income that nearly doubled British salaries between 1958 and 1966, which raised the standard of living and turned mods into keen consumers. Mod men preferred an urbane, inter-national look of dress borrowed from the Italian style of *La Dolce Vita*, French café culture and the American Ivy League. New-found affluence allowed them to spend their money on Italian suits with thin lapels and tapered trousers. Their girl-friends adopted Brigitte Bardot hairstyles, heavy eye make-up and knee-length skirts to wear while pillion-perched on their boyfriend's Lambretta or Vespa scooter. The mods' lives were centred around fashion and music, and the boutiques and dis-cotheques were their meeting places.

In French, *boutique* simply means 'shop', but in the 1930s the word had taken on a stylish connotation in English when some Paris couturiers created outlets to sell accessories and scents. Christian Dior understood the power of luxury shop-ping when his Paris boutique carried a growing range of Dior-brand merchandise in the 1950s, including cosmetics, corsetry, scarves, shoes and hats. The shop served the couture business by promoting the Dior name, but also became a resource for finding future couture clients, who started as avid boutique shoppers. In the US, the word 'salon' was used as a near equivalent for 'boutique'. Hattie Carnegie had the most famous salon, offering a variety of ready-made fashions and accessories alongside in-house custom dressmaking

services. The leading English designers who were engaged in couture in the 1950s, Norman Hartnell, Hardy Amies and John Cavanagh, had only a small roster of bespoke clients. Britain was still recovering from wartime debt and reconstruc-tion, and few British women could afford the extravagance of couture. Designers relied upon alternate sources of income, including export sales, film costuming, ready-to-wear lines for department stores and menswear, but had not yet taken up the idea of opening boutiques to sell their own lines of high-end ready-made clothes and accessories.

'Boutique' was still a foreign concept in the UK when Alexander Plunket Greene and his business partner Archie McNair opened Bazaar in November 1955 on King's Road in Chelsea. Plunket Greene's girlfriend, Mary Quant, was hired as the first buyer for Bazaar, and with his encouragement she soon began selling her own designs – often made up from adapted Butterick patterns the night before. Plunket Greene and Quant were married in 1957, the same year the business was expanded to include a second location, in tonier Knightsbridge. Quant's shops were hits with London's 'bright young things', who liked the informal, youthful, American beat-influenced fashion for dark tights and English schoolgirl-style pinafores (jumpers), or Brigitte Bardot-inspired gingham dresses and low-heeled shoes. Quant offered no couture services; her shops carried 'a bouillabaisse of clothes and accessories', as she wrote in her 1966 autobiography, *Quant on Quant*.

Quant led the way in what became known as the 'Chelsea look', which was at the forefront of the changing fashion scene for young British designers who were starting boutiques around the same time: John Stephen opened his first men's shop in Carnaby Street in 1957; John Michael followed with his first men's boutique in 1958; John Bates began designing under the Jean Varon label in 1959; Sally Tuffin and Marion Foale started working together in 1961, although they didn't open a boutique until 1963; Jean Muir, who had worked for other labels includ-ing Jaeger, launched her company Jane & Jane in 1962; and

THE MOD'S MONTHLY

1'6

APRIL

FASHIONS
for the
FUTURE

TWO-PAGE
EXCLUSIVE by
CATHY
McGOWAN

SHOES · HATS
COATS
RECORDS
DANCES

MODS IN
YOUR AREA

Page 33: Twiggy,
December 1966.

Left and opposite:
The Mod's Monthly,
a publication for mods
living outside of London,
first published in March
1964. Front covers,
April and May 1964.

EXCLUSIVE
ARTICLES
BY
CATHY
McGOWAN
and
VICKI
WICKHAM

SHOES · HATS
COATS
RECORDS
DANCES

MODS IN
YOUR AREA

Kenneth Street, Gerald McCann, Kiki Byrne, James Wedge, Roger Nelson and others all opened around that same time.

Millicent Bultitude, the author of *Get Dressed*, a guidebook to London's boutiques in 1966, defined a boutique as 'a small informal shop, probably run by the proprietors, selling mostly exclusive fashionable clothes and accessories'. In recognition of Mary Quant's leading role in the creation of the boutique movement, Bultitude had Quant write the foreword. Quant inexplicably penned, 'I hate boutiques. It is a pity because the Bazaar which we opened in the King's Road, Chelsea, in 1955 is the grandmother of all the little shops – both good and bad...that have sprung up in London and sell original and amusing clothes in an original and amusing way.'

For autumn 1962, Dior picked up on an English aesthetic with schoolboy-inspired striped wool suits and scarves with the style names 'Soho' and 'Chelsea', both worn with matching fabric caps. The American junior fashion industry also took notice of how well the 'Chelsea look' was doing; in 1962 Mary Quant was commissioned to create a line of clothes for one hundred JCPenney stores in forty-four US cities. The response was not as positive as hoped – prices were high and the styles lacked hanger appeal. Paul Young, who had arranged for the experimental imports with JCPenney, admitted to *New York* magazine in 2003 that when setting up the boutique Paraphernalia, 'Clothes of this type don't look like anything on racks.' To resolve the cost problems, Quant created the Mary Quant Ginger Group Wholesale Clothing Design and Manufacture Company to streamline production. American sales dramatically improved on the second try in 1963, and Quant continued to design two collections a year for JCPenney well into the 1970s. Ginger Group fashions by Quant were soon being sold around the world.

In 1963, London's *Sunday Times* gave Mary Quant a special prize in the first of its International Fashion Awards for 'jolting England out of its conventional attitude towards clothes'. Doris Salinger, fashion coordinator for Bloomingdale's in New York, said in an interview with the *New York Times* on 3 June 1964, 'The English were so conservative for so long that all designing talent was crushed.... Suddenly the young people began going into business for themselves.' Many noted that the youthful fashions were a revolution, mirroring the anti-establishment literature of Britain's angry young writers. Geraldine Stutz, president of upmarket retailer Henri Bendel, noted in the same *New York Times* article, 'What John Osborne did in drama is now happening in fashion.' *Life* featured some of the leaders of the 'nonconforming young fashion designers' in its 18 October 1963 edition: 'They are not mad. They are just irreverent, out

Far left: Low-cut evening dress designed by JOHN BATES for JEAN VARON, London, *c.* 1964. The low neckline, high waistline, straight skirt-style evening dress was one of Bates's most successful designs that he reissued for several seasons.

Left: Cathy McGowan modelling new looks in the first edition of *The Mod's Monthly*, March 1964.

Below: 'The Young London Look' interpreted for the Canadian market by Simpsons-Sears, autumn 1965.

Opposite left: 'Zingy London Look': English styles interpreted for the Canadian market by Eaton's, spring 1966.

Opposite right: Japanese youth wearing mod fashions, September 1966.

A really with-it Suit obtainable from Woodlands, 21 Shop, Knightsbridge, in Pink with Navy Blouse; Mauve with Pink Blouse; Navy with Gold Blouse and Green with Pink Blouse. Style 647
Price £7 19 6

Cathy McGowan, who models all the dresses shown on this page is seen below in a smart dress she has designed herself.

For the really Mod look a dress also available at Woodlands, 21 Shop, Knightsbridge, in Plum, Yellow, White and Blue. Style 605.
Price 6½ Gns.

the young LONDON look

to shake up traditional British fashion.… In business only a few years, this giddy group has already become a major style influence in England. And they are catching on with young Americans, who can now buy their moderately priced clothes in scores of US cities.' Louis Constantine, buyer for the Young New Yorker department at Lord & Taylor in New York, which carried Mary Quant clothes, noted in the *New York Times* article of 3 June 1964, 'They do not look home made any more and they are certainly influencing Seventh Avenue.' Paris couture had always been a laboratory where style was created before it was sent out into the world to become fashion. Boutiques were now operating in the same way as couture but in reverse, working their way up the fashion ladder, inspiring higher-end designers to copy popular looks

The most ardent customers of boutique fashions were the mods. The British television programme *Ready Steady Go!*, which featured performances by popular mod bands, aired between August 1963 and December 1966 – the height of mod culture. A contest to find a youth advisor for *Ready Steady Go!* was won by Cathy McGowan, who ended up as an on-camera presenter of the show. Twenty-year-old McGowan's fashion sense quickly won her the honorary title of Queen Mod. When she went to New York in February 1964, a Vancouver, Canada, newspaper reported: 'Over in England they have a Queen Mod.… I saw her the other day when she was flown to New York for a TV show.… The queen's followers are also known as "mod" and if they became enthusiastic about anything it is described as "fab". Cathy McGowan is the real name of the Queen Mod and she earned her title when she was chosen from 1,000 applicants to be the teen age interviewer on a British record and dance program called *Ready Steady Go!*.… What she wears is Mod law…her female followers never wear lipstick, hair is to be worn straight, and shoes are to be "granny".… The mod girls change their fashions quite frequently but are currently employing ankle-length skirts for street wear, which may be an indicator of what we'll be seeing soon in this part of the colonies when the fashions spread from Mod Queen's Court…. The dispatches indicate that there is a restlessness among the stylists and the clothes wearers and that fads, fab or not, are apt to change quickly. While long dresses are now a must, they could whip up to mid-calf or knee in the twinkling of a beaded eyelash.'

When McGowan returned to England she wrote about her impression of American youth fashions for the May 1964 edition of *The Mod's Monthly*, a publication that had just debuted in March: 'American fashion has remained static. The boys are wearing their conventional sweat shirts and jeans just as they have been for ages, they do wear these sneaker shoes which I suppose is a slight break from convention but their hair is still crew-cut except for a few who are attempting to grow Beatle cuts…. I think the Liverpool four are great, but who would walk down the street with their faces imprinted on the front of whatever you're wearing. Then there are Beatle wigs – you know the things they sold over here to have a giggle at a party with – well, they wear them in the streets…that's the thing to do you know. The girls…wear "everest" high-heeled shoes, colourful dresses and lots of make-up. No one it seems can be bothered to step out of line and try to create an extremely new outfit. It's no wonder that they thought I was from another planet…. They haven't heard of Mods over there, but they were fascinated by my clothes…. I get the idea that they think as Beatles are British, then British fashion must be equally the thing to have….'

However, while mod fashions were crossing the Atlantic to America, some American fashions were being sent back, as McGowan reports in the June issue of *The Mod's Monthly*: 'I expect you notice that I've been wearing jeans and sweat shirts…. I think this style will be "in" for most of the summer because even we know that there's nothing worse than going down [to] a club and absolutely baking in a wool suit! If you want to buy really smashing jeans that really fit well go to a boys' shop for them – John Stephens have really smashing hipsters in denim (pale blue look great, or white)…. The boys' outfits are the same as the girls' – tee-shirts, sneakers and jeans. Lots of boys have started to wear dark blue denim "Levi's" but these must really fit on the hips or else they look completely wrong.'

Life tried to explain how mod style came to America in a September 1965 article entitled 'British and Dizzier Than Ever': 'The clothes made by the brash new breed of British designers made the US scene along with the Beatles and so far as fashion was concerned, their impact was just as great. They brought kooky, ebullient styles: "Chelsea" collars – a low scoop, "mod" skirts – above the knee or at the ankle, any place but the usual, and outrageous colors and patterns suitable for "birds" – cute girls. They were so promptly and widely copied that a swift demise was predicted. The giants of the US ready-to-wear industry now think otherwise. They have imported the young British designers themselves to do this fall's clothes…. Their styles have already totted up sales figures in the millions, and look to be at least as durable as Ringo Starr.'

Back in the UK, Cathy McGowan continued to lead young mods in and out of fads that would last weeks, or a month or two at most: grey sweaters, round glasses, gloves, leather jackets, tweed jackets, crochet collars, airline bags, bowling bags…mods had to keep with it or else become a 'first-class ticket' (a clueless unfashionable). In October 1965, McGowan announced that she would launch her own line of mail-order fashions in early 1966 for the benefit of mods not living near the latest boutiques. Her business lasted into the early 1970s.

Mods flocked to the brick-and-mortar boutiques of London, as well as those in other towns like Manchester, in search of fun, affordable clothes – and to meet friends. The most successful boutiques created a party atmosphere where the clothes seemed hipper because they were sold to the sound of the latest song, and chicer because it was where the top celebrities also bought their clothes. However, many of the boutique clothes were poorly constructed to make them affordable for the young clientele; single-stitched seams, machine finishing,

Above: Blue-and-purple print shirtwaist dress by TWIGGY, London, c. 1967. Twiggy launched a line of clothes produced under her name in November 1966; the line was dissolved in early 1970.

Left: Black leather-like finish nylon raincoat by CATHY MCGOWAN, c. 1968.

raw selvedges and cheap textiles that tended to shrink, run and pill during cleaning were common problems with boutique clothes. The focus was fun and affordable for a fast turnover – trends changed so quickly that there was a good chance last month's purchases would be out of style by the time they came back from the dry cleaner.

While mods were influencing fashion in the English-speaking world, in France it was the *yé-yé* girls – Françoise Hardy, Sylvie Vartan, France Gall and other young singing sensations named for their 'yeah-yeah' choruses who were setting the mode with *le style anglais*. France was still largely a nation of dressmakers, but American-style designer ready-to-wear and young boutiques were on the rise. The fans of the *yé-yé* singers became the locomotives of young French fashion, flocking to the boutiques and department stores.

A 12 September 1965 *New York Times* article relates how Brigitte Bardot was approached by Coco Chanel to become a client: 'Dress at my house and I will make you into an elegant woman,' she said. To which Bardot replied, 'Elegance? I couldn't care less. It's old-fashioned.'

Street clothes were in, and the movement for 'off-the-rack' turned into a fashion for looking poor; boiling sweaters to make them doll-sized became a popular trend in 1965 that crossed the Atlantic to the US, where *Life* noted on 14 May 1965 that there was 'More girl than sweater...short sleeves and bare midriff to look like it's shrunk.' At Prisunic, a chain that in the 1960s had over 300 stores throughout France (as well as Spain, Greece and North Africa), young women loaded up on shift dresses and cheap T-shirts printed with target designs (the origin of what would become the logo T-shirt trend).

Opposite: Suede suits by French leather and suede clothing company MAC DOUGLAS, Paris, spring 1965.

Right: The 'poor-boy' sweater worn with miniskirt, Paris, 1967.

Far right: Vicky Tiel in her studio, Paris, 1965.

Le Drugstore and Elle were also popular boutiques for cheap chic; for girls with a bit more cash the favourite Paris boutique was Réal. The owner, Arlette Nastat, had been carrying chic ready-made clothes since 1956 for Paris's young set and had many celebrity clients, including *yé-yé* girl Sylvie Vartan, and actresses Brigitte Bardot and Catherine Deneuve. By autumn 1964 a line of clothes from Réal was being made in the US by Andrew Arkin and sold under the label Mademoiselle Arlette. German playboy millionaire Gunter Sachs's boutique chain Micmac (French slang for 'chaos') opened in 1965 and was especially successful after his marriage to Brigitte Bardot the following year. Celebrity was good for sales, as young American designers Vicky Tiel and Mia Fonssagrives realized. The two arrived in Paris in 1964 with no experience and little money, but they did have a couple of solid connections that hurtled them from unknown fashion-school grads to star boutique owners. Mia Fonssagrives's mother had been a famous model in the 1940s and 1950s; her stepfather was fashion photographer Irving Penn. Upon arriving in Paris, Mia met and fell in love with couturier Louis Féraud, and she and Tiel were given the opportunity to design pieces for his collection. They then designed costumes for Woody Allen's first film, *What's New Pussycat*, in 1965, and were soon partying with the jet set, including Elizabeth Taylor and Richard Burton. The Burtons financed their boutique venture, Mia + Vicky, which became a favourite among young French and American women visiting the city.

The stars of Paris ready-to-wear included Emmanuelle Khanh, a former model for Balenciaga who began designing her own clothes in 1960. 'Couture is dead. I want to design for the street,' she said in an interview in the 13 March 1964 issue of *Life*. While she admitted Balenciaga's and Givenchy's clothes were beautifully cut, she felt they looked more expensive than pretty. In 1962 she teamed up with fellow former Balenciaga model Christiane Bailly to produce an off-the-peg collection under the label Emma Christie. Other favourites of

ready-made fashions included the young knitwear designer Sonia Rykiel; Dorothee Bis, who had six franchised boutiques across Europe by 1966; and Michèle Rosier, daughter of the publisher of *Elle* magazine.

Haute couture was not oblivious to the changing world. The three most influential French designers of younger styles in the 1960s, Pierre Cardin, André Courrèges and Yves Saint Laurent, all moved into ready-to-wear to find success and influence. Cardin was the first, in 1959, and Courrèges and Saint Laurent followed in 1966. When Yves Saint Laurent opened his first Rive Gauche (Left Bank) boutique on rue de Tournon in Paris that September, he noted in various interviews that his true public were young working women who led very different lives from those who wore couture, and that not all of the young would want couture, even if they could afford the high price.

An autumn feature on young-style clothes in the *New York Times* on 25 October 1964 came with the warning: 'There's no point in mincing words. The bald truth is that fashion leadership is being usurped by youngsters…a totally new attitude has captured design on both sides of the Atlantic. France's zippy *yé-yé*s, the British neo-Victorians, and Rudi Gernreich, the daring American, are major contributors to the new mood, which is a heady brew of astute tailoring, Jazz-Age heirloom and moon travel. Those over thirty should sample with caution.'

Acknowledging the power of the youth revolution that was occurring, American *Vogue* editor-in-chief Diana Vreeland wrote in the 1 January 1965 issue: 'There is a marvelous moment that starts at thirteen and wastes no time. No longer waits to grow up, but makes its own way, its own look by the end of the week. The dreams, still there, break into action: writing, singing, acting, designing. Youth, warm and gay as a kitten yet self-sufficient as James Bond, is surprising countries east and west with a sense of assurance serene beyond all years. First hit by the surprise-wave, England and France already accept the new jump-off age as one of the exhilarating realities of life today. The same exuberant tremor is now coursing through

'The Accent is Paris': ANDRÉ COURRÈGES and YVES SAINT LAURENT interpreted for the Canadian juniors market by Eaton's, spring 1966.

the accent is paris

1 Contemporary costuming in nubby textured linen-weave rayon. The dress, a slim sheath topped with double-breasted jacket dipping into a deep U-front. The outfit bound for contrast. Skirt fully cotton-lined, with kick-pleat, buckled self belt. 70 (White/Navy); 75 (Black/White). 41-K 2254B. Misses' sizes 10 to 18 . . 16.98 For hat information, see page 55.

2 The mood is Mondrian! Sleeveless shell of a dress in bold squares of white, green, red graphically defined in black; back solid green. 80% Orlon, 20% wool jersey bonded to acetate. Self belt. 46-K 5555A. Misses' sizes 10 to 16 . . 14.98 Along geometric lines, the "toque" hat in the same material. 4-K 3328. One size fits to 22½ inches 5.98

3 Charted in white, the straight-forward lines of our water-repellent all-weather coat of Canadian Mist (cotton and nylon). White rayon lined. 48 (Navy/White); 37 (Blue grass Green/White). 44-K 4054B. Misses' sizes 8 to 16 . . 19.98 Matching 'kerchief hat fits all sizes. Water-repellent. Elasticized back; self bow. 4-K 4313C. 70 (White); 48 (Navy) . . 3.98

6 EATON'S

YOUNG JUNIORS
Teen sizes 8 to 16.

Heather and Hound's-tooth

Be courageous—switch on in mix and match co-ordinates

Left: American floral-print
cotton-blend trouser suit,
UNION label, *c.* 1966.

Below: American green
suede shoes, *c.* 1965–66.

America – which practically invented this century's youth in the first place. The year's in its youth, the youth in its year. Under 24 and over 90,000,000 strong in the US alone. More dreamers. More doers. Here. Now. Youthquake 1965.'

The word 'youthquake' aptly described the sudden onset and lingering aftershocks the fashion world would experience from the younger generation making its mark on mainstream style. The 1966 French film *Who Are You, Polly Magoo?* satirized the obsession with youth – proclaiming in a voice-over of a montage of contemporary fashions by Courrèges, 'Fashion was once for the rich, but now it's just for teenagers…. Little-girl fashion, no chest, no hips – just knees, socks, flat shoes, little boots…. Androgynous Little Red Riding Hoods and itty bitty women.'

American department stores had featured junior fashion departments for almost thirty years, but they were adult-approved spaces where teens could shop with their mothers. They were focused on school clothes and sportswear: sneakers, jeans, windbreakers and button-down shirts for boys, with stretch trousers, 'boyfriend' shirts, oversized sweaters and jumpers for girls. American youth fashions lacked the dressy town clothes of mod style, or the street chic of the *yé-yé* girls. They could dress like kids, but there wasn't a sophisticated way for them to dress up without looking like their mothers had clothed them.

Paul Young, a British expat who had been working for JCPenney since the mid-1950s, felt there was room for a boutique style approach to selling youth fashions in the US. Young was the reason Mary Quant had been approached in 1962 to sell a line of fashions through the store. There wasn't any interest from JCPenney to open a special boutique, so Young approached Carl Rosen, the president of the stodgy-sounding Puritan Fashion Corporation. As Puritan already had the licence to make Beatles T-shirts, Rosen liked the idea of a youth boutique and hired Young to head a new division at Puritan called Youthquake.

The first goal of Youthquake was to reach the market for under-twenty-fives across the US, which was only 15 per cent of Puritan's business at the time. In 1965, Paul Young and Carl Rosen signed three-year contracts with Mary Quant and Foale & Tuffin to design for five of Puritan's brands: Barnsville, Carousel, Young Naturals, JP's, and Paddle and Saddle. These brands were available in department stores across America. Puritan commissioned the song 'Youthquake' and had it recorded by The Skunks; to promote sales, a 45-rpm record of the song was given away with every purchase of Puritan's mod-design fashions.

The next step was to create a flagship London-style boutique that would grow into a national chain store selling hip clothes for young people. There were already boutiques in the US by 1965, such as Splendiferous and Serendipity in New York, but Young and Rosen's Paraphernalia was aiming to stock a more comprehensive selection than any existing store. On 1 October 1965, the first Paraphernalia opened at the corner of 67th Street and Madison Avenue, next door to Vidal Sassoon. The interior of the shop was conspicuously modern with curved steel, chrome, multi-levels and white walls. The music was loud enough to keep the older generation and 'squares' away; sometimes there were even girls go-going in the window. It felt like there was always a party going on.

Music was essential for the hippest boutiques. The month before Paraphernalia opened in New York, Mary Quant and fellow London-based designer Caroline Charles were touring the US promoting their new American-made lines, Quant with Puritan and Charles with Jonathan Logan. Both designers unveiled their collections at 'happenings' that included go-go dancing models and live music. 'What the kids want is music and clothes. Every store in England that sells my clothes plays the music all day long,' said Charles in a *New York Times* article on 2 September 1965. Quant agreed, adding that she was the first to realize music and mod clothes were inseparable and had been playing music in her boutiques since they had opened.

During the first few years, Paraphernalia had a stable of contributors including French designer Emmanuelle Khanh and British designers Mary Quant, Foale & Tuffin and Veronica Marsh, with shoes by Moya Bowler and hats by James Wedge. American designers included Carol Friedland, Jonathan Hitchcock, Camila Smith, Michael Mott, Elisa Stone, Diana Dew, Walter Holmes, Deanna Littell (who had received a Coty Award for Young Designers of 1965), Betsey Johnson (who had been working in the art department of *Mademoiselle* magazine) and Joel Schumacher (a store window-dresser who would later go into costume design and film directing). Many of the American designers worked in-house, in a huge studio that fostered creativity. They all had freedom to develop their designs – the motto was 'anything goes', as long as it ultimately sold. Because the clothing was made in small lots, the designers could take risks with styles, fabrics and processes. Deanna Littell used fluorescent purple and green leatherette to make raincoats with glow-in-the-dark white inserts and details, with matching miniskirts to be worn with buffalo-checked taffeta cowboy shirts. Emmanuelle Khanh created a do-it-yourself no-sew dress of suede strips attached to each other by dome fasteners so the client could have any length of skirt she wanted. Betsey Johnson became known for her silver tinsel evening dresses inspired by Edie Sedgwick, who frequented Warhol's silvered interior factory space, but Johnson also came up with kookier ideas, like a see-through vinyl dress for $15 that came with packs of adhesive-backed foil pieces for an extra $5 that could be applied in any pattern. Walter Holmes created the 'Medieval Mini' that was shown with a wimple in the fashion columns, making the models look like nuns in miniskirts – the Catholic Church was not pleased.

All the clothes were designed exclusively for the Paraphernalia label, and nothing was priced over $100. One of the few exceptions was a $150 vinyl dress designed by Diana Dew

TIME WAS WHEN EVELYN NESBITT WAS THE FIRST SWINGER

Swinging dress in soft, see-through purple with lots of kaleidoscope dots. Michael Mott's floating idea for **Paraphernalia**®. About $40. Old England's watch for all-time swingers with moiré velvet band in five colours. $16.

Paraphernalia

Above: Advertisement from US *Vogue* for OLD ENGLAND brand lady's wristwatches and PARAPHERNALIA dress with angel wing sleeves by MICHAEL MOTT, May 1968.

Right: Walter Holmes's 'Medieval Mini' for PARAPHERNALIA, 1968.

that lit up with the aid of a battery-pack belt. The reality of fashion for the young was that they didn't have a lot of money and profit had to be made through volume sales by keeping trends moving through the store at a dizzying pace. Style was more important than substance with Paraphernalia's fashions, which often had the same poor quality issues as many of the British boutique clothes. In 1966, *Harper's Bazaar* called it 'enjoy-it-today-sling-it-tomorrow' fashion.

Paraphernalia was radical for its time. 'You have to realize how square everything was,' recalled Joel Schumacher in an article for *New York* magazine in 2003. 'When we opened, women were still wearing hats and gloves. There was even a union rule that no dress could be shipped unless it was a certain length.' The shop was open until midnight three days a week, something unheard of at the time, and quickly became the hottest boutique in the country. Plans to expand, mostly

by opening satellite shops within department stores across the country, were immediately put into action.

Twiggy, who had rocketed to fame as a top model in the UK during 1966, arrived in New York on 20 March 1967 to promote London designs sold through hip boutiques such as Tiger Morse, Teenie Weenie, Abracadabra and, of course, Paraphernalia. In just eighteen months since Paraphernalia had debuted, there were nearly thirty branch locations across the country, popularizing trends like oversized wristwatches with coloured wristbands, floppy felt hats, wide belts and men's ties. Surrounded by the press in New York, Twiggy's first stop was at Paraphernalia where she met Betsey Johnson. This kind of attention didn't sit well with the old guard of New York fashion. Mainbocher termed the sort of clothes Paraphernalia turned out as 'slang fashion' – amusing but lacking the basic grammar of style. Johnson was aware of her privilege in being able to

Left: 'A-Foot' ankle boots with zippers by MARY QUANT, London, 1967–68.

create as she wanted, but she was also aware of what some in the industry thought of her clothes when the venerable Parsons School of Design refused to let her speak to its students.

Regardless of the old guard's view of the boutique generation, *Time* magazine pointed out in a December 1967 article that 'at the boutiques, where the prices are low, the taped rock music is loud, and the amateur salesgirls just can't resist breaking into a frug while waiting on customers…. Boutiques are now being shopped by everybody, from teen-agers and secretaries to Jackie Kennedy. She picked up half a dozen bush shirts for her recent trip to Angkor Wat at Manhattan's Paraphernalia.'

Jax was another influential boutique, first having opened in Los Angeles in 1944 and by 1952 carrying clothes by Rudi Gernreich. By 1965 Jax had expanded to an eight-store chain stretching from Beverly Hills to Manhattan. It was popular for its young-style, easy-fitting casual clothes, from jeans and T-shirts to simple, sexy slip dresses. The store was also known for its aloof salesgirls and their studied disregard of customers. 'Too many young adults dress too old,' said the store's creator and owner, forty-six-year-old Jack Hanson, in a *Life* article in October 1965. 'They should dress as casual and young and functional as possible. And live that way. If you're going to act old at thirty, you might as well forget it.'

Riding the wave of young design, the Coty American Fashion Critics Awards were presented in autumn 1965 to nine up-and-coming designers: Edie Gladstone, Victor Joris, Stanley Herman, Sylvia de Gay, Leo Narducci, Don Simonelli, Gayle Kirkpatrick, Bill Smith and Paraphernalia's Deanna Littell. 'Females are too fickle today – they don't want to invest a fortune in clothes they will be tired of next year,' explained Edie Gladstone in a *New York Times* article covering the awards in September. 'It's the fun of wearing clothes that is most important today,' added Sylvia de Gay.

In London, Chelsea was still the centre of the women's fashion scene, even though the city was awash with boutiques – some the 'size of a telephone box' joked *Queen* magazine in 1965. The December 1966 printing of Millicent Bultitude's guide to London boutiques included Alice Paul, Annacat & Co., Biba, The Carrot on Wheels, Early Bird, Fifth Gear, The Gloryhole, Just Jane, Palisades, Pelisse, Quorum, Scope, The Shop, Swag, Thirteen A, Top Gear, Troubadour, Victoria & Albert, The Yellow Room, Zanie and many more. However, London was no longer the only place where chic young styles could be found. Boutiques were popping up all over the UK; in Manchester some of the top shops included Pygmalia, Baines, The Toggery, George Best and Crowthers. For men, Carnaby Street was still an important shopping road in London, but by 1966 it was becoming choked with gawking provincials and tourists.

Department stores in the UK had by now clued in to the boutique movement. In 1966 they began carrying affordable runs of boutique-style fashions under brand names like Dollyrockers and Quad for 'store within a store' departments that were decorated to bring the boutique spirit to a larger customer base, in the same way as Mary Quant's clothes were being sold through JCPenney in the US.

By late 1966, mod had peaked in popularity and was on the decline. Mod had always embraced a neo-Romantic look in women's fashions: crocheted lace collars, 'granny' shoes, ankle-length hems and knit suits mixed nostalgia with modern materials and youthful styling. By autumn 1966 a more fearless outbreak of nostalgia was beginning to show in fashion. Even Mary Quant conceded that mod clothes were 'trying too hard' and said her autumn collections would feature classic English styles and materials like tweed pleated skirts.

The television programme *Ready Steady Go!*, which had been the sound of mod, ceased airing in December 1966 because the music scene was changing, fragmenting and moving in different directions. The next wave of fashion was going to be ruled less by boutiques and more by the leading musicians of trendsetting bands.

Two films aptly captured the era. The English comedy *Smashing Time*, released in 1967, was an insightful satire about

Right and far right: Blue rayon tie dress by MARY QUANT, London, spring 1968, and models wearing the dress in London, with Quant herself on the right, March 1968.

Swinging London just as the mod trend had passed its peak. Two girls from the north of England, Yvonne (played by Lynn Redgrave) and Brenda (played by Rita Tushingham), arrive in London seeking excitement, fame and fortune, but hapless Yvonne doesn't realize she is behind the times in her plastic raincoat and bouffant hair, while serious Brenda, with her straight hair and vintage granny nightgown, accidentally becomes the next new thing. Caught up in the glamorous world of celebrity, ultimately the girls realize there is no place like home. The other film, *Blow-Up*, released around the same time, had a more serious tone. The story was inspired by the lifestyle of British mod fashion photographers such as David Bailey, who gained fame in the 1960s when modelling and photography were transformed into glamorous and lucrative careers. The film is not kind to the British mod fashion culture, depicting how the pursuit of freedom became the pursuit of pleasure and, without discipline, turned to decadence.

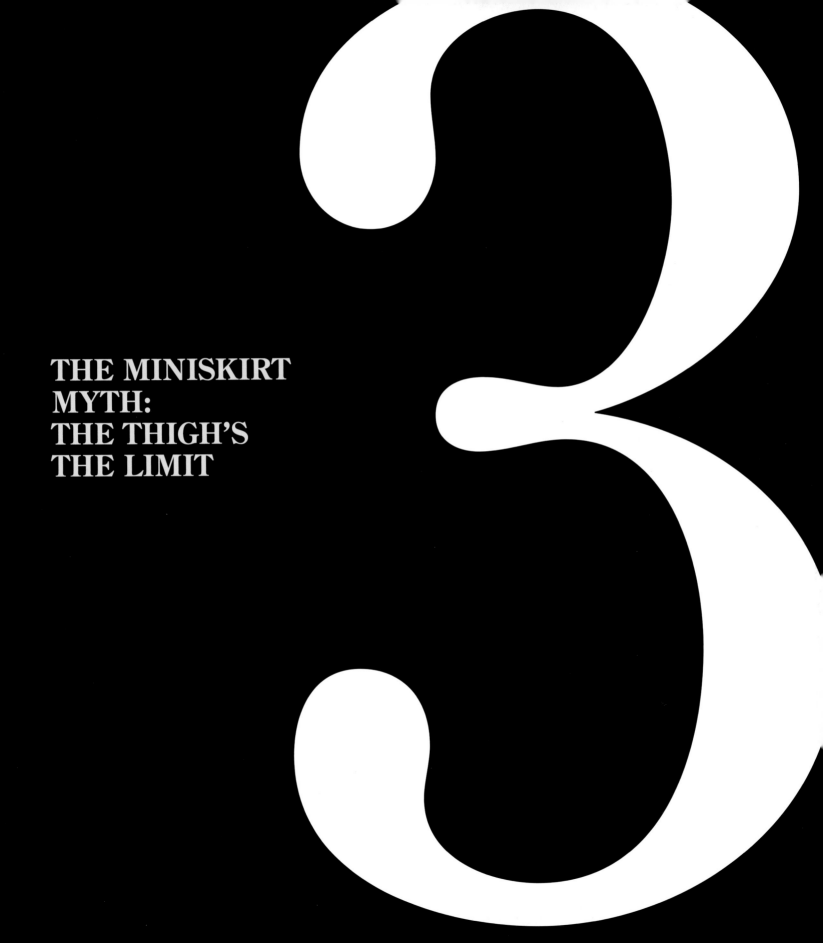

THE MINISKIRT MYTH:
THE THIGH'S
THE LIMIT

'It wasn't me or Courrèges who invented the miniskirt anyway – it was the girls in the street who did it.'

Mary Quant, quoted in *Couture* by Ruth Lynam, 1972

By the 1960s little girls had been wearing short skirts for generations, and women had been wearing above-the-knee shorts at the seaside and for sports activities since the 1930s. During the Second World War, American teens regularly wore skirts an inch or two above the knee in the name of patriotic austerity, especially while dancing the jitterbug. However, the hemline always remained below the knee for town wear. Some felt it wasn't proper to expose knees in polite society, while others felt that knees were just ugly. 'There was a time when women always had to wear long or three-quarter sleeves because they said their elbows were ugly. They've learned to live with ugly elbows and don't give them a thought any more…. Women will learn to live with ugly knee joints and won't give a damn,' said Norman Norell in a *New York Times* article in March 1966. Some fashion designers felt the knob of the kneecap broke the line of the leg's curve, and that 'just below the knee' was the most aesthetic length. Coco Chanel, whose famous suit

style was a triumph for women who wanted to disguise figure flaws, was quoted in a September 1965 *New York Times* article as saying the bare knee was 'everything that is most ugly in a woman…. Have they all gone mad?'

The first inkling that short skirts were being worn in town appeared in a snippet in the *New York Times* from July 1962: 'The sleeveless shift or muumuu, cut loosely and ending several inches above the knee, is appropriate for wear at a beach or even on the streets of a resort. Its popularity, however, has now extended to Manhattan streets, a fact that is deplored even by the designers who promoted it.' The muumuus being referred to without doubt include the dresses offered by Marimekko for summer 1962 that *Life* featured in an article on 15 June: 'Muumuu, or shifts, or Marimekko…by any other name this year's popular straight-hanging, figure-concealing dress is distressingly the same shape as the sack. The Marimekko, a Finnish import whose name is derived from an old word

Page 54: Fifteen-year-old British actress Susan George, late 1965.

Right: Eaton's catalogue, Canada, summer 1970. Mid-thigh miniskirts were revolutionary in 1965 but by 1970 the style had become so prevalent that it was hard to convince younger women that they should wear anything longer.

Right: Knee-length 'Flutterby' print cotton shift by VERA, New York, spring 1963.

Below: Above-the knee shift by RUDI GERNREICH for JAX, California, May 1962.

Opposite left: Skirts a little below the knee for town, and a little above the knee for country in *Seventeen* magazine, November 1962.

Opposite middle: This image from an unknown publication is captioned: 'New styles for the grown-up girl by LINZI were shown in London this morning. They include culottes – knickerbockers and mod-Victorian cotton shifts.' 23 November 1964.

Opposite right: Sitting bared the knees in all just-below-the-knee hemlines, like this dress by JACQUES ESTEREL, Paris, spring 1964.

meaning little girl's dress, is becoming an enveloping fad…. Made of hand-screened cotton prints, it is sometimes with flounces or yokes, but it is always unfitted through the waist. Matching tie belts are provided for the timid but usually wind up on the wearer's hair instead of around her waist.'

In California, Jax, the influential chain of boutiques that specialized in sportswear including designs by Rudi Gernreich, also offered above-the-knee shifts. A May 1962 Jax advertisement in US *Vogue* showed a model in an urban setting wearing an above-the-knee chemise, suggesting it could or should be worn in town.

Thirteen- to twenty-five-year-olds constituted a third of the American population in the early 1960s, and the fashion industry tracked what this demographic was buying to forecast trends – including a noticeable preference for shorter hem lengths. Teen fashion magazines *Seventeen* and *Mademoiselle*

often featured skirts and jumpers with above-the-knee hems in the early 1960s. A *New York Times* fashion feature for teens from July 1963 suggested, 'For playtime, the wrap skirt and the culotte, knee-length or shorter, are taking over…', and in September, Saks Fifth Avenue advertised plaid jumpers that were above the knee in length.

When measuring hem lengths from the knee there was confusion as to whether to include all or part of the three-to-four-inch kneecap itself. Adding to the problem, fashion photography of the period frequently obscures the length of the hem. Models are usually shown in some pose where they are slouching or standing in a manner that causes the skirt to rise. Even when sitting, a below-the-knee hem length rides up above the knee.

In November 1964, English designer John Bates illustrated what he thought would be the 'little girl' silhouette for spring

Left: Knee-baring wool suit by
COURRÈGES, Paris, autumn 1964.

Opposite left: The 'granny' hemline,
twelve inches from the floor, was
popular with mods in the winter of
1963, and continued to show up in
designer collections after mods had
abandoned longer hems during the
spring of 1964. This striped chiffon
evening shift by FRANK USHER was
featured at a fashion show of British
styles in Berlin, 19 October 1964.

Opposite middle: Top-of-the-knee
cocktail dress by PATRICK DE
BARENTZEN, Paris, autumn 1964.

Opposite right: Just-below-the-knee
dress by VALENTINO, who was never
a fan of above-the-knee hem lengths,
Rome, autumn 1964.

1965 with a sketch for the *Daily Express* that showed a model with a hem two to three inches above the top of the knee. However, Bates's fashions for spring 1965 were generally more modest than his sketch.

Paris designer André Courrèges's 1964 couture collection was reported as showing hemlines two inches above, which was true if you measured from the middle of the knee. The Courrèges hem length bared the knee, but no thigh. Because of this, Courrèges is often given credit for the invention of the miniskirt because, as a Parisian couturier, he had the attention of the international fashion press. His work gave the above-knee hemline high-fashion credibility. In London, Mary Quant, as the figurehead of a coterie of young designers who created the mod 'Chelsea look', is also given credit with inventing the miniskirt; however, all dated images of Quant fashions show knee-length skirts into 1964 or, alternatively, the 'granny' skirt, with a hemline twelve inches from the ground in early 1964. London 'Mod Queen' Cathy McGowan was advocating Quant's skirt and even wore a couple on her trip to New York in February 1964. However, a couple of months later McGowan announced in the April 1964 issue of *The Mod's Monthly* magazine, 'Well, at long last, long skirts are on the way out. They were great though while they lasted, quite the weirdest thing on the scene for months, but sooner or later they had to go. Hemlines have now got back to civilization. Best dressed stylists have settled for straight, knee length skirts, preferably in black or navy.'

In the spring of 1965, Courrèges moved the hemline up on some of his dresses to four inches above the middle of the knee, which now exposed a flash of thigh with every step. Less than three years earlier, when women had worn their summer resort shifts in the streets of Manhattan, there was

outrage from the fashion press, but now there was a growing acceptance.

Spring 1965 saw the onset of what US *Vogue* dubbed the 'youthquake' (see page 47). Fashion was offering simple shifts and 'little girl' dresses, inspired or made by London designers. The hems were at the top of the kneecap and were shown with knee socks or coloured tights and flat shoes. The shorter hem looked appealing and innocent with young, slim legs – not overtly sexual, until some young women began hemming their dresses shorter and shorter to show off their leggy assets. In a *New York Times* article from September 1965, Quant commented that her line of American fashions made by Puritan were being made too long, and 'now everybody is turning them up so they're several inches above the knee'.

With Mary Quant and the rising hem constantly in the fashion news throughout 1965, the two became inextricably linked. The following year, when the miniskirt was ubiquitous, Courrèges and Quant would both be credited with its invention. But Quant has said on many occasions that 'the birds went on putting them up in spite of me', referring to her customers, who hemmed up their skirts regardless of the length at which Quant sold them. In an interview with author Ruth Lynam for her 1972 book *Couture*, Quant said, 'It wasn't me or Courrèges who invented the miniskirt anyway – it was the girls in the street who did it…. Maybe Courrèges did do miniskirts first, but if he did no one wore them.' Fellow designers Sally Tuffin and Marion Foale agreed in an interview with the Victoria and Albert Museum in 2006, saying, 'It wasn't that Mary [Quant] did anything or that we did anything – it was all those kids that pushed the boundaries.'

The largest hurdle to pass in the creation of the miniskirt had been baring the kneecap, for aesthetic and etiquette reasons. Several designers played a part in pushing hems up to and beyond the kneecap, including Mary Quant, André Courrèges, Rudi Gernreich, Marimekko and John Bates, as well as many lesser-known designers. However, once the knee had been breached, it was the young women buying the dresses who shortened the skirts, taking hemlines higher and higher during the summer of 1965 until they had created the thigh-high miniskirt. Of all the fans, mods seemed to be the most crazed for the fashion, and the style quickly became associated with Swinging London, where the shortest hems could be found.

On 30 October 1965, British model Jean Shrimpton stepped into a fashion maelstrom when she attended Derby Day at Flemington Racecourse in Melbourne, Australia, with no hat, no gloves, no stockings and a hem four inches above her knees. The rapid changes in fashion that had occurred that year were suddenly very visible on the tall, leggy model, and the reaction from Australia's conservative establishment illustrated how not everyone had yet acclimatized. The twenty-two-year-old model was one of the 'faces' of Swinging London and was on a well-paid tour of Australia to promote a range of Orlon dresses made by a local manufacturer. The dress was sent to the five-foot-nine-inch Shrimpton before the event but, as she recalled in her 1990 autobiography, 'The day of the races was a hot one, so I didn't bother to wear any stockings. My legs were still brown from the summer, and as the dress was short it was hardly formal.'

The incident was reported by the Australian media and quickly picked up worldwide. Melbourne's mayoress Lady Nathan suggested, 'If Miss Shrimpton wants to wear skirts four inches above the knee in London, that's her business, but it's not done here. I feel we do know so much better than Miss Shrimpton…we all dress correctly here.' Supporting Shrimpton, the *Evening News*, London, retorted that 'surrounded by sober draped silks and floral nylons, ghastly tulle hats and fur stoles, she was like a petunia in an onion patch'.

The miniskirt became a topic for debate that touched upon issues such as the generation gap, the changing times and the future of fashion. Appearing at her next function, Melbourne Cup Day on 2 November, Shrimpton wore a three-piece grey suit

Above: Jean Shrimpton wearing a miniskirted suit at Melbourne Cup Day, Australia, 2 November 1965.

Right: Dress with indeterminate hem length by COURRÈGES, Paris, c. 1967–68

Left: 'Thigh-High Invasion from England' reads the caption for this news photo from 12 August 1965. The two women photographed at a New York discotheque wear matching turtleneck sweaters and tights with thigh-high miniskirts.

Opposite: Women with novelty designs painted on their legs, 1966.

Far left: Pink nylon windowpane stockings, unlabelled, *c.* 1966–68

Left: TWIGGY mesh stockings by Simpsons-Sears, Canada, spring 1968. With the leg so exposed, more patterned stockings, featuring designs from ankle tattoos to windowpane mesh, appeared on the market.

Opposite: Advertisement for COTY BODY PAINT, July 1967. For some summer fun, leg paint and decals, available at cosmetics counters and novelty stores, could be applied to bare legs.

The idea of Body Paint. Crazy!

No body who loves mini, kicky, bare-as-you-dare fashions looks dressed without it. (Coty Originals gives you a *face* for every fashion, and now a *body* too.) So roll on the Body Paint. Go green, blue, mauve. Or try a flesh tone (pick from four). Delicious pearlized colors leave skin gleaming. Smooth. Even covers flaws. Non-smeary. Stays on 'til you soap-and-water off. Can of Body Paint, complete with roller and pan. 6.00. Comes with all three colors. Or one flesh tone.

Betsey Johnson for Paraphernalia.

Coty Originals
what big ideas you have!

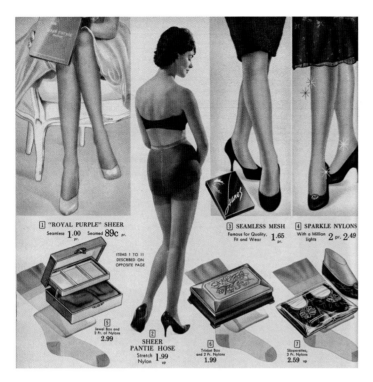

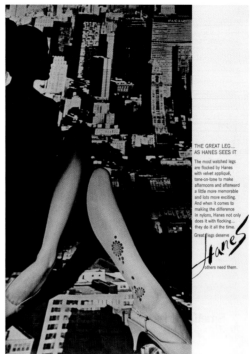

with an ice-blue straw Breton hat, and beige gloves and stockings. Speaking to reporters, Shrimpton jibed, 'I feel Melbourne isn't ready for me yet. It seems years behind London.'

As is often the case in fashion, one year's outrage turns into next year's rage, and the miniskirt was no exception: 1966 would become the year the mini took off. Mary Quant wore a mid-thigh minidress in June 1966 to receive her Officer of the Most Excellent Order of the British Empire (OBE) from the Queen, in recognition of her contribution to the British fashion industry. The British news establishment flustered over the protocol – was Quant's skirt indecent?

Even though Quant didn't solely invent the miniskirt, she is often credited for naming the style after her favourite car, the Mini Cooper, which she once called the 'handbag on wheels'. However, her 1966 autobiography, *Quant on Quant*, which never discloses any dates, also doesn't use the word 'miniskirt' – not

even once. The word began to appear in late 1965: an advertisement for a $3.69 'Mini Skirt' in the *Bakersfield Californian* newspaper was published on 19 August, and on 10 October Montgomery Ward advertised in Pampa, Texas, a sale of turtleneck dickey and stocking sets to be 'worn with mini-skirt or shorts'. The word was in common use by the time it appeared in the *New York Times* on 29 May 1966, where it is used casually and familiarly in a humorous rant about spring fashions from Britain: 'The mini-skirt can be a thing of splendor, provided the woman wearing it does not weigh more than 89 pounds and is blessed with the legs of a hosiery model. On all others it is the stuff of tragedy,' wrote Russell Baker.

Public, private and parochial school boards contemplated how short a hemline should be allowed. The resulting rules ranged from mid-kneecap to a few inches above, calculated by whether the skirt touched the ground when kneeling,

Opposite left: Advertisement for stockings and pantyhose, Simpsons-Sears, Canada, autumn 1961. Pantyhose, a sheer version of tights, were first marketed in 1959 and gained popularity along with the rising hemlines during the 1960s.

Opposite right: Advertisement for HANES tattoo ankle designs, 1965.

Right: Making news in early June 1965, the Dean of Girls at Del Vallejo Junior High School in San Bernardino, California, enforced a school dress code that required thirty-five students to sew crêpe-paper extensions onto their skirts, lowering the hemlines to the top of the knee.

or if the hemline was higher than the tips of the fingers. Of course this didn't stop girls from rolling up their waistbands when the teachers weren't looking. On 13 August 1966, Tunisia announced a ban on miniskirts, becoming the first of many countries to ban skirts above the knee that would eventually include most of the Islamic world and the Vatican.

'How Much Higher Will They Go?' asked *Life* in an April 1966 issue: 'Legs are getting longer than ever, and especially in swinging old England…[London] has become the undisputed capital of the thigh-high skirt.' The *New York Times* asked several women how they felt about the new fashion for short skirts in an April feature. The designer Anne Klein said, 'I never budge without a scarf, which I try to drape across my knees without looking as if I were setting a table.' Mrs Henry Newfeld, wife of a theatrical manager, replied, 'I've shortened my skirts about an inch since last summer, but I won't go above

the top of the knee – that's enough if you're over twenty-five.' Jackie Zimmerman, a young copywriter, responded, 'I guess my skirts are three inches above my knees – I'm quite used to them short.' A year and a half later, in December 1967, *Time* magazine ran a similar feature and found little had changed – forty-one-year-old Manhattan socialite Marylou Whitney never wore skirts higher than one inch above her knees, while fellow Manhattan socialite, twenty-six-year-old Wendy Vanderbilt, felt that 'the thigh's the limit' with her skirts.

Designers' reactions to the miniskirt were mixed. The *New York Times* quoted British designer Norman Hartnell's reaction to mid-thigh hemlines at a 'Young Britain' fashion show at the B. Altman & Co. department store in New York in March 1966: 'I find them cute, uplifting and sunny – I really do, but there's no beauty in them at all.' American designers James Galanos and Norman Norell expressed similar reactions in the

Left: Navy-and-white-striped skirt suit by CHRISTIAN DIOR, spring 1968. Hemlines were now varied according to the preference and age of the wearer. Just above the knee was typical of middle-aged women who were not comfortable with hemlines halfway up their thighs.

Above: Wolf whistles for the miniskirt
in Chicago, late summer 1966.

Left: Red wool minidress by
GEOFFREY BEENE, *c.* 1966–68.

Time magazine article from December 1967. 'All they've done is chop five inches off the hem and they call it new. To me it's a laugh,' said Galanos. 'Elegance is out,' sighed Norell. 'It's a fascinating, frustrating time to be a designer.' Most designers, whether pro- or anti-mini, resorted to offering most of their skirts and dresses in lengths designed to terminate around the knee, allowing customers to raise the hem to their own preference.

By autumn 1967, many younger Seventh Avenue designers were showing mini lengths for older women. Chester Weinberg, aged thirty-seven, who had just started under his own label in early 1966, became one of the more successful new designers to adapt mini styles for more mature women by making his clothes from high-end materials. Jacques Tiffeau, forty, showed the shortest skirts of anyone on Seventh Avenue (eight inches above the knee) but softened the look by using flowing silks. Oscar de la Renta, thirty-four, best known for his evening gowns, went romantic with a group of dresses in white organza and lace petals. Bill Blass, forty-five, admitted that in 1966 he went for young customers and ignored his old clientele, designing the most extreme collection of his career, which included see-through bodices. Blass quickly realized he had to get off his youth kick if he wanted to stay in business, and for 1967 he showed dresses three inches above the knee, but in black with lots of lace and ruffles and high necklines.

The general consensus was that a true mini rose to mid-thigh level, but as there seemed to be no end to how high the hem would go, new categories would be invented. One San Francisco designer jokingly told *Time* magazine in December 1967 that 'there is the micromini, the micro-micro, the "Oh, My God" and the "Hello, Officer".' What surprised so many in the fashion business, from journalists to designers, was

Very "now" for individualists
Junior petite sizes 7P to 15P

EATON'S 21

Far left: Brown lace cocktail dress for the conservative mini-wearing woman by CHESTER WEINBERG, New York, *c.* 1967–68.

Left: 'Granny' gown by Eaton's, Canada, autumn 1966. In October 1965, *Life* magazine reported how teenage girls in Los Angeles were wearing floor-length dresses instead of minis: 'California kids are wearing long hemlines for fad's sake…in cotton with high waistlines…they call them hostess dresses but never wear them at home. They look like "Hawaiian muumuu gone Chelsea mod" and wear them to the beach, movies, Disneyland, but not, as yet, to school.'

Opposite left: News photo of Los Angeles teens wearing 'granny look' long gowns, 19 October, 1965.

Opposite right: Cotton 'granny' gown by ANNE FOGARTY, late 1960s.

the apparent lack of inhibition that many women displayed in wearing miniskirts. Gloria Emerson, a journalist with the *New York Times*, commented in February 1968: 'Girls with thick ankles, knock knees and chubby thighs wore the mini-skirt as assertively as females with the long racehorse legs of a Dietrich. They knew it didn't flatter them and they didn't care.'

The mini was more than a hemline that grabbed the attention of men; it was a way of rebelling against protocol. As part of the 1960s social revolution, the mini became a symbol of change in fashion that toppled the old establishment. It suppressed prudery and brought power to a new generation of young stylists who were plugged in to the here-and-now tastes of youth. Young, modern women wanted to look striking, sexy, vibrant and wild, and they wanted their clothes to be carefree, unbinding, colourful, kooky, liberating and revealing.

SCANDAL SUITS AND SHAPELESS SHIFTS: THE MID-1960s

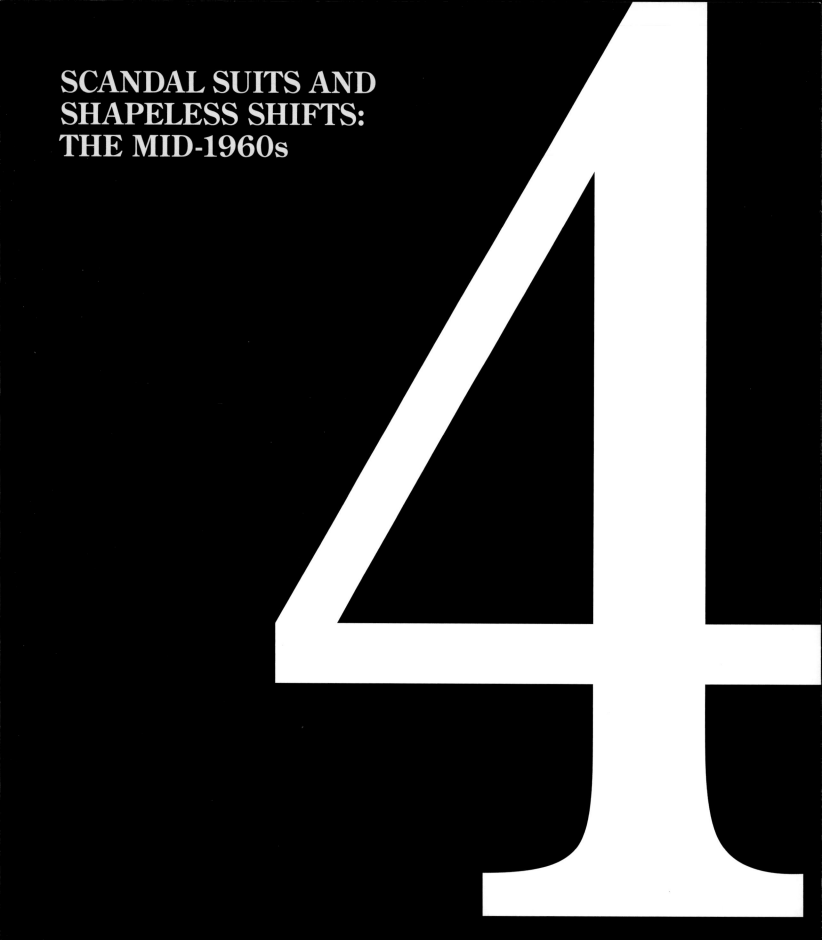

'Chic women…have smorgasbord fashion appetites. They may buy a few ball dresses in Paris, a suit from Valentino, hostess pajamas from Rome….'

Marilyn Bender, *New York Times*, 1 August 1965

In the spring of 1964 André Courrèges was creating fashion headlines with his conspicuously modern collection of perfectly tailored haute couture clothes. Probably his most-photographed item was a white suit consisting of a small-sleeved, low-necked, hip-length doublet worn over sharply creased straight white trousers, slashed at the instep to accommodate white kidskin boots. Every seam was welted, accentuating the straight and narrow shape of the trouser legs. His lithe little white dresses also featured long, lean legs in hemlines that stopped above the knee.

In Paris, prints were scarce and white was the new black, although navy, revived by Yves Saint Laurent the previous spring, was popular. Marc Bohan for Dior had a hit that spring with a navy-blue dress that featured a pleated silk skirt and bell-sleeved bodice cut low to feature cleavage. He called the model 'Tom Jones' after the previous year's eighteenth-century bosom-filled film hit of the same name. *Life* commented on the sudden appearance of cleavage in its 3 January 1964 edition: 'After four years of riding high, necklines are plunging…. They are the forerunners of a trend that is strong for spring.' The fashion prediction was right, and as spring turned to summer, 'Tom Jones' décolletage appeared in more dresses, often with an empire silhouette, underscoring the historic wench reference.

Where bareness stopped in dresses, bathing suits stepped in. Though it had been popular in locales like St Tropez for years, the bikini was slow to catch on in the US, even after Sandra Dee had paved the way for its acceptance on American beaches. It was teen-movie queen Annette Funicello and her on-screen girlfriends wearing belly-button-baring two-piece bikinis in a series of 1964 surf-and-sand movies who really paved the way for the bikini to take over.

The fashion cause célèbre of summer 1964 was Rudi Gernreich's monokini: a topless knitted bathing suit consisting of a pair of high-waisted trunks with shoulder straps. However, the style was never intended as a serious fashion. It started when a *Women's Wear Daily* reporter asked Gernreich about bathing-suit trends. He predicted that in five years American women would be removing their bras to sunbathe, just as French women were already doing on the Riviera. Gernreich created a sample for an editorial in *Look* magazine, showing what a bare-breasted swimsuit might look like if the style were to become acceptable in the future. Word spread, the fashion press buzzed, department stores placed orders and Gernreich put the suit into production.

The public reacted with every possible emotion, from leering fascination to moral outrage. *Time* magazine carried reports of irate women picketing stores that sold the topless swimsuit, brandishing signs that read: 'AS MOTHERS WE PROTEST TOPLESS SWIM SUITS' and 'WHAT NEXT?' Newspapers and magazines fuelled the controversy by speculating throughout the summer how there were going to be monokini-only bars and beaches. Ministers railed from their pulpits. 'Just two straps closer to the moral decay of America,' declared the Reverend Jacob Belling of the Neighborhood Church in Oakland, California. Public beaches and pools banned the topless fashion even before Lee Shelley, a nineteen-year-old publicity-seeking model, briefly wore one on a Chicago beach before being arrested.

Hess Brothers department store in Allentown, Pennsylvania, ordered twelve suits and had one on display for curious customers to see the shocking style for themselves. Recognizing a good gimmick, Irwin Greenberg, the store's president, told the press they had sold out and were reordering. Hess's became famous overnight and line-ups to see the suit grew longer. The publicity didn't improve monokini sales, but it brought customers to the store, where they spent money in other ways – buying $10 men's shirts or lunch in the restaurant that boasted a state-wide-famous strawberry pie. At summer's end Hess Brothers had not sold one monokini; the stock was liquidated through Filene's bargain basement in Boston for $2.50 each. The suit inspired cartoons with tag lines such as, 'Bikini sale, half off!' Very few of the 3,000 suits made by Gernreich actually sold at full retail; the design was a failure, but the publicity was priceless – Gernreich was famous.

The topless bathing suit excitement was still raging when it was reported in the *New York Times* on 22 June 1964 that British manufacturer Carnegie Models Ltd, recognizing the value of controversy, was making bare-bosom cocktail dresses that were on sale in London dress shops for $15. Miss Rae Southern, a 'dancer', was hired to wear one of the dresses, with tassel-less pasties, to a restaurant, accompanied by a reporter and photographer from the *Sunday Mirror*. She was quoted in the article: 'The manager very politely asked me to leave.... He said I was causing embarrassment to his clients. But…the waiter who served in the restaurant didn't bat an eyelid when he took our order.' In the same article Mary Quant was said to be coming out with two topless dresses in September 'that she wouldn't mind wearing' herself, although those designs never materialized.

Rudi Gernreich returned that autumn with his version of a transparent shirt, made in shiny black chiffon. Henri Bendel in New York carried Gernreich's transparent top for what it called 'private lives', not intended for public viewing. Bill Blass created black lace dresses with nude-coloured linings for autumn 1964. Teal Traina, as well as Bill Smith for Roban, designed sheer-bodice evening dresses; however, these used a layer or two of flesh-coloured chiffon with a sheer black chiffon outer layer, so the nudity was more illusive than real. For the shy, Warner's in the US and Canada created a flesh-coloured body stocking designed specifically for these kinds of nude illusion garments, although English designer John Bates was quoted in the *Daily Sketch* in December 1964 as saying, 'No woman should wear a foundation, they're ugly and uncomfortable.'

The dalliance with nudity inspired designers to play with illusion, including mesh fabrics and cutouts in dresses.

In London, John Bates for Jean Varon designed trousers with cutouts on the knees called 'keyhole kneeholes', as well as a dress with a fishnet midriff he called the 'Ad Lib'. Cole of California also used fishnet panels in a bathing suit designed for its winter 1965 resort collection, dubbed the 'scandal' suit: the panels exposed considerable flesh and cleavage, but the most important bits remained covered by opaque nylon spandex.

Journalist Shana Alexander wrote about her experience buying one of these bathing suits in the 7 May 1965 edition of *Life*: 'Last week half the racks were choked with bikinis, and the rest dripped enough black mesh, veiling and fishnet to make me think a school of tattered mermaids had just molted there. These were the so-called 'scandal suits'.... They are the logical fashion evolution of…the topless bathing suit, and they give the illusion of bareness, which of course is always better to look at than the real thing. As Yogi would say, they are smarter than the average bare.'

Topless and transparent garments were never going to be a serious mainstream fashion, but the free press garnered from the controversy encouraged intentionally provocative looks in future collections. If designers failed to create controversial or edgy styles, fashion magazines stepped in, commissioning pieces for photo editorials of which many were identified as being available to the public, even though they were not.

Paris generally continued the tradition of precise tailoring for autumn 1964 fashions. White was still the new black, and skirts were hemmed at the knee and worn with wildly patterned or lacy stockings. Coats and capes were cut close to the body and worn with low-heeled boots, laced shoes or suede pumps.

Suits had swing in them, often because of pleated skirts that promoted movement. Courrèges's collection included double-faced skirt suits, beige on the outside and white on the inside, with double-breasted jackets over wrap skirts two inches above the knee, as well as trouser suits cut the same for day and evening but in white lace for after five.

Although not as dramatic as the debate over nudity, there was controversy over women wearing trousers and where they should be worn. Women had been wearing pyjamas and slacks for casual and sportswear for decades, but now these were being suggested for high fashion. For autumn 1964, London mod designers Sally Tuffin and Marion Foale created sporty corduroy day suits. American designers Pauline Trigère, Hannah Troy and Anne Klein showed evening trousers cut so full that they looked like skirts, while Norman Norell showed slim-cut trousers intended for travel and country wear. In Paris, Courrèges was suggesting trousers for day and evening, cut slim to the leg, which had *Life* asking in its 23 October issue: 'Pants...are they suitable for sophisticated social rounds in the city?' The most successful trouser styles were by Russian-born Italian designer Princess Galitzine, who had for several years been creating trouser ensembles for evening parties at home, or in other people's palazzos. The full-legged but clearly bifurcated style was known as 'palazzo' trousers, and became a big hit for autumn. The fashion spread to New York via Paris, where several designers, including Chanel, Jacques Heim and Guy Laroche, created jewel-trimmed palazzo-trouser evening ensembles for the 1964 holiday season. Evening jewelry – necklaces, brooches and bracelets – moved towards the dramatic, with bigger, heavier and more colourful pieces, especially earrings – more women were now having their ears pierced to better wear the long, dangling styles.

Spain was beginning to be noticed as a fashion source by 1964. Designers Balenciaga and Castillo had been influential for years, but their work came out of Paris – Spain's fashion industry had been stifled by the isolationist economy that had followed its Civil War in the 1930s. Those working from Spain had few opportunities to showcase their designs abroad until the mid-1960s, when the economy was becoming stabilized. The most successful of these was Manuel Pertegaz who, in 1958, was the first Spanish designer to sell internationally to Lord & Taylor in New York and I. Magnin in Los Angeles. Herrera y Ollero, a design house founded in Madrid in 1952, found success when it promoted its fashions at the 1964 New York World's Fair, landing a deal with department store Bonwit Teller to carry its clothes that autumn; Elio Berhanyer struck a similar deal that season with Bergdorf Goodman. Within a few years Spanish fashion, especially leather goods, would become influential around the world.

Far left: Advertisement for palazzo trousers by GALITZINE, Rome, June 1963. The style would become a very popular and much-copied hit for the 1964 holiday season.

Left: White wool pantsuit by COURRÈGES, Paris, autumn 1964.

Opposite left: Open-sided evening gown with beaded waist and hem by HEINZ RIVA, Rome, *c.* 1965–66.

Opposite right: French cotton dress with bare midriff, labelled 'LUIS – MARI, NICE, CÔTE D'AZUR', *c.* 1966–67.

Above: Colour-block vinyl boots, sold through Sears department stores, *c.* 1965–66.

Above right: Black-and-white Op art-print slingback pumps, *c.* 1965–66.

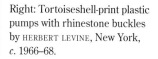

Right: Tortoiseshell-print plastic pumps with rhinestone buckles by HERBERT LEVINE, New York, *c.* 1966–68.

Below: Coat dress by GALITZINE, Rome, spring 1965.

Right: The COURRÈGES influence is visible in tailored culottes and boots by ANTONELLI, Rome, spring 1965.

Above: GEOFFREY BEENE's 'little girl'
look of oversized collar and bow
sailor dress, New York, *c.* 1965–66.

Right: Pop art necklace-print
cotton dress, sold throughout
the US, spring 1965.

In the 1 January 1965 edition of the *New York Times* a review of 1964 fashion outlined the year's highlights: Courrèges trouser suits, smock dresses from young British designers, swinging shoulder bags, a 'poor' sweater from the French new wave, a Vidal Sassoon cropped haircut, wild eye make-up with one or more pairs of false lashes, lace and patterned stockings, and nude illusion dresses with transparent bodices. 'No great fashion came out of 1964 but everyone had a lot of fun,' exclaimed the article.

Hemlines in New York's spring 1965 collections were slightly shorter than in the previous season – on or just above the knee was becoming common. Originala, a conservative Seventh Avenue coat manufacturer, struck out into suits for the first time with skirts hemmed an inch above the knee. Gernreich rose the highest, showing dresses up to three inches above the knee. Regardless of length, suits were often shown with white or off-white coloured stockings and low-heeled shoes. Coats were straight and generally two or three inches above the knee; for foul weather, shiny opaque vinyl raincoats were popular. American improvements in plastic vinyl inspired Parisian ready-to-wear designer Michèle Rosier to create space-age raincoats, spurring an interest in the material for fashion use that grew throughout 1965 and 1966.

Emilio Pucci recognized that evening entertainments were changing and fashions needed to adapt. In a *Life* article from 16 October 1964, Pucci said, 'My feeling is that the old evening dresses, heavily embroidered, bedecked with ribbons and flounces, are beautiful for receiving somebody at the foot of the stairs. But if the wearer starts dancing the cha-cha or the twist she looks positively ridiculous.' As Pucci predicted, several designers showed short evening dresses for discotheques in their spring 1965 collections, but long, straight gowns in strapless and one-shouldered looks remained popular for formal evening events. In the US, chiffon was a popular material for one-shouldered gowns; in fact, American fashions in general tended to be softer than Parisian, in line and fabric.

Courrèges's spring 1965 collection was again a favourite with fashion editors – his spare style was now recognizable and influential, but not yet cliché. Courrèges's palette was still largely white. His accessories were as admired as his clothes; enormous slitted white sunglasses and open-toe bow-tied boots were well received for spring. However, it was his hemlines that were most noticeable – he was pushing for shorter skirts, four inches above the knee. London mod styles were also baring the knee and inching up the thigh during 1965, igniting a debate over who invented the miniskirt. 'It's ridiculous to focus on hem lines. Wearing my clothes is a question of spirit,' said Courrèges in an interview with *Life* for the 21 May issue. Along with the rising hemline, Courrèges also refused to have his models wear brassieres, 'which in ten years will be as forgotten as whalebone corsets are today', or to show high heels, which he said were 'preposterous…. Boots are a more feminine solution and more rational and logical.'

By the summer of 1965, shapeless shifts had become popular, and they were the perfect canvases for Pop and Op art prints. Pop art glorified everyday objects, usually on an over-sized scale, while Op art was about creating dazzling patterns and three-dimensional effects. The shapeless dress remained in fashion for several years, with floral and psychedelic patterns eventually displacing Pop and Op prints. The shapeless shift also inspired the 'little girl' look of the mid-1960s: kindergartener dresses with smocking, bows and puffed sleeves, worn with low-heeled Mary-Janes and white knee socks or stockings; a Breton hat completed the look of innocent gawkiness.

With fashion looking younger, older, established designers and manufacturers mattered less. In a 22 February 1965 article in the *New York Times*, New York manufacturer of high-end dresses Harvey Berin lamented, 'Where is the better dress business going to…. Last year, I had a…drop in sales, the first…since I started back in 1922…. Young women today – particularly the suburbanites – have a different image of how they want to look…a more relaxed outlook on fashion.'

Adding to the troubles of changing tastes were higher labour and material costs. In a similarly themed article from the *New York Times* on 27 December 1965, manufacturer Larry Aldrich pointed out industry challenges: 'The problems of the better price, or the couturier-type producer have centered on three basic elements – the narrowing of demand, the inroads by imports and the increasing lack of skilled workers.'

Founded in 1953 as an association to represent and promote New York manufacturers of high-end dresses, suits and coats, the New York Couture Group had by now become irrelevant to newer manufacturers who were not applying for membership, such as Malcolm Starr, which opened in 1961. The dwindling group joined up with the American Fashion Business Council to become the New York Couture Business Council Inc. in February 1966, but its effectiveness as an influential business organization deteriorated over the next five years as many of the old member companies, established in the 1940s or before, closed. Many owners were of an age that allowed them to retire gracefully, like Max Pruzan, who quietly resigned his partnership with Monte-Sano, a coat and suit manufacturer since 1932. Some owners realized they couldn't adapt to how the business had changed; Arthur Jablow, for instance, closed down his company, and his designer David Kidd moved over to Originala. When interviewed about why he chose to close his thirty-seven-year-old business, Jablow admitted he was 'quitting when I'm ahead.... Fashion is changing – women want car coats, knitted suits, suede coats and raincoats,' he observed in the *New York Times* on 8 April 1966. Pruzan and Jablow both expressed concern that the demand for expensive clothes had not kept pace with the affluence of the times.

Rising in the New York Couture Group's place was the Council of Fashion Designers of America (CFDA), rallied together by New York fashion industry publicist Eleanor Lambert in 1962. Lambert had also been the catalyst for the creation of the New York Couture Group. She created the CFDA when she saw that the industry was no longer a trickle-down hierarchy of couturiers and manufacturers. Lambert correctly anticipated the rise of the small designers and the power of their creative force within the industry. Among its objectives, the CFDA lobbied for recognition of fashion as an art form, entitling the industry to federal government support.

The Incorporated Society of London Fashion Designers, better known as 'Inc. Soc.', was in a similar situation, stuck in the old ways of how fashion worked: from the top down. Established designers of high-end fashion were becoming irrelevant; 'Inc. Soc.' lost influence during the 1960s to the boutique movement, and disbanded in 1970.

Paris was also realizing that ready-to-wear was the future of fashion. The French couture industry was in crisis, having been without government subsidies since 1962, and the younger generation didn't have the time, patience, money or desire for fitted clothes made with interlining, boning or any kind of figure-altering construction. Fashion had to be modern, affordable and easy fitting. Since the late 1940s Dior had maintained luxury boutiques that carried accessories and semi-couture ready-to-wear requiring one fitting, but Pierre Cardin created an even more American-style ready-to-wear line for the Printemps department store in Paris in 1959. After his spring 1965 couture collection Courrèges claimed he would only design ready-to-wear. In an interview with *Life* that appeared in the 21 May 1965 issue he said, 'Soon I should have the possibility and the means to dress the women who do not have the means to dress in original Courrèges. Working women have always interested me the most. They belong to the present, the future.... My couture house is my laboratory.... My creations must also enter the industrial phase. It remains the most important part of our venture.' Courrèges had no haute couture collection for autumn 1965, and he didn't manage to pull together an 'off the peg' collection in time either. However, a line of leather clothes designed by Courrèges exclusively for leather manufacturer Samuel Robert was available that autumn.

Right: Printed cotton shift by DYNASTY, Hong Kong, *c.* 1965–67.

Far right: Beaded discotheque dress, made in Hong Kong, by MALCOLM STARR, *c.* 1965–67.

The following year, Yves Saint Laurent would follow by opening his boutique of ready-to-wear fashions designed to appeal to the younger set, named Rive Gauche (Left Bank), after the bohemian section of Paris where his first store was located.

For American clothing companies, there was a stampede to the stock market, as smaller firms went public with the idea of growing into corporate giants with multiple clothing divisions. The best way to weather lean economies, sudden changes in taste and market mistakes was to have broad industry representation in everything, from sportswear and junior lines to high fashion and underwear. Manufacturers Jonathan Logan,

David Crystal and Russ Togs were the first to grow to megacorporation proportions; Jonathan Logan took the lead with twenty-three divisions ranging from knitwear to raincoats.

In an effort to keep their prices low, some companies were shifting to offshore production in places such as Haiti, Trinidad, Panama, Japan and Taiwan. Japan and Taiwan were sourced specifically for their combination of advanced technology combined with affordable labour that kept export prices low. Both countries specialized in producing inexpensive fashion lines in synthetic materials, as well as accessories and novelty items in a range of plastic and rubber substances, from jewelry and

umbrellas to sandals and sneakers. Synthetics were constantly being improved to imitate more expensive materials; glazed nylon and wet-look vinyl were especially convincing in their resemblance of kid and patent leather – from a distance.

In 1964, designer Urleene Chaplain was hired by Dynasty to create a cheaper line of fashion in Hong Kong using textiles other than silk, which the company had been using exclusively. Capitalizing on this, Italian designer Patrick de Barentzen was brought in to design half the future dress lines of Dynasty in 1966. The clothes no longer simply followed Chinese styling, but rather used the expertise of Hong Kong hand labour to reproduce high-fashion European-style clothes. De Barentzen, commenting in a 1967 interview, said of a $200 jewelled yoke shift made by Dynasty from his design, 'That would cost $1,500 in my salon. I don't see how they can do it.'

Marilyn Bender reported on the autumn Paris couture collections in the *New York Times* on 1 August 1965: 'The showings got off to a listless start last Monday.... The buyers and reporters from all over the world...strained to detect something new.... [Lanvin] had reduced its collection by one half, closed three of its five workrooms and acknowledged that it was showing fashions only to promote the sales of its perfumes, the most famous of which is Arpège.' Bender went on to report that there was little new at Dior and even Balenciaga showed nothing that would compel women to invest in his clothes. 'There are the giants like Dior, and the top trio in

Opposite: Geometric-print suits by
<small>VALENTINO</small>, Rome, autumn 1965.

Right: Geometric-print suits by
<small>BALESTRA</small>, Rome, autumn 1965.

Far right: Wool coat with Op art
pattern designed by <small>EVERETT STAPLES</small>
for <small>JEAN PIERCE</small>, Toronto, *c*. 1965–66.

terms of prestige with American buyers and socialites – Balenciaga, Givenchy and Saint Laurent. The rest of the haute couture establishments are shrinking to the status of private dressmakers, or are vehicles for the promotion of perfumes and accessories....' Bender recognized that modern women were no longer following one lead in fashion: 'Chic women… have smorgasbord fashion appetites. They may buy a few ball dresses in Paris, a suit from Valentino, hostess pajamas from Princess Galitzine in Rome, hats from Halston of Bergdorf Goodman in New York, something in leather from Spain, and frilly cottons on a sojourn in Mexico.'

With Courrèges absent from haute couture for autumn 1965, Yves Saint Laurent was the stand-out favourite at the shows. His bold Mondrian-inspired dresses of ivory wool jersey with black outlines of colour-blocked sections in bright red, yellow or blue were especially well received. Many designers in Paris and elsewhere were influenced by Op art and showed geometric black-and-white chequerboard-inspired prints. Emanuel Ungaro, former assistant to Courrèges, launched his label in this season, showing short-jacketed suits with dirndl skirts, heavily influenced by Courrèges's clean tailoring style with welted seam detailing. For evening, most French gowns showed a more romantic side, often made of lace – some with feathered trimming, like those by Pierre Cardin. Nightclub clothes went down the shimmery route, including silver cloth; Capucci even showed luminescent beadwork that glowed in the dark.

Aside from Yves Saint Laurent, and the British mod looks, American designers were getting more coverage in American newspapers, particularly Norman Norell and James Galanos,

Opposite left: Grey-and-white wool dress and coat set by JACQUES HEIM, Paris, c. 1965–66.

Opposite middle: Looped wool dress by SAMUEL WINSTON, New York, c. 1965–66.

Opposite right: NORMAN NORELL yellow silk crêpe 1920s-inspired drop-waist dress, New York, c. 1966–67.

Right: American wool dress with Op art midriff panel, label removed, 1967.

Far right: Velour ski jacket with Op art pattern inspired by Victor Vasarely's *Orion*, Canada, c. 1966–67.

who were especially revered by the fashion press as being as good as anything coming out of Paris. The American look for autumn was heading in a new direction that involved influences from many sources. Coats were still very tailored, but dresses and suits were moving away from the sharply fitted Courrèges-influenced Paris styles of the previous few seasons. There were more sweater dresses worn with hip belts, and separates – leather skirts paired with simple sweaters or blouses, inspired by the *yé-yé* girls of Paris and Britain's mods. Dresses with matching accessories – hats, spats or socks – or sweater, dickey and tights for a unitard look, were shown by different designers. The Courrèges-style shin-high boot was now being worn everywhere, although shoes were still more popular, especially sandals and slingbacks, which were being worn well into winter, often with solid coloured tights including black,

as favoured by Warhol 'superstar' Edie Sedgwick. Handbags were shrinking while jewelry was still growing in size – huge dangling earrings that touched the shoulder or a pendant necklace were favourites.

Norell and Blass were not embracing the youthquake for evening clothes, preferring to show more conservative fashions, including glittering beaded and sequined jackets or cardigans over simple dresses. Geoffrey Beene went younger, showing slinky but covered-up dresses, while some designers aimed at very youthful styles – Galanos and Sarmi showed evening gowns that were either strapless or featured bare midriffs.

The *New York Times* summed up the leading fashions for 1965 in its 31 December year-end review: 'This was the year of the go-go girl who needed clothes to keep going…. The year was a bullish one for…Bill Blass (prince of the ruffles and the baby

Above: Rayon scarf with Op art
pattern in the style of British
artist Bridget Riley.

Right: One-shouldered bathing suit
with Op art pattern by SEA QUEEN,
Canada, c. 1966–67.

Right and far right: Inlaid patterns on shift dresses by PIERRE CARDIN, Paris, spring 1966.

Below left: Chevron-stripe suit and coat by YVES SAINT LAURENT, Paris, spring 1966.

Below right: Chequerboard suits by JACQUES HEIM, Paris, spring 1966.

dress) and…Paris couturier Yves Saint Laurent who lost his shyness, found Mondrian…. Among the newer faces of 1965… are Deanna Littell and Luba Marx, American representatives of the international youth movement in design that was called Ye-Ye in France and Mod in Britain; George Stavropoulos, the Athenian whose chiffon dresses kept popping up in…socialite wardrobes…Ken Scott, the American fabric and sportswear designer…. Vidal Sassoon, the London hairdresser, also looked at women with a geometric vision…the most important men in a fashion-oriented woman's life were her hairdresser, her make-up artist and Kenneth J. Lane – the king of counterfeit jewellery who made mammoth fake earrings…. Watch out for more sun visors by Halston who sparked the scarf hat fad, unconstructed dresses and floppy coats, the downgrading of suits…. We haven't finished with teenagers, pierced ears, boutiques, nudity as a fashion concept, and…women won't think twice about going anywhere in pants.'

The year 1966 was characterized by conspicuous modernism. Dazzling prints inspired by Pop and Op art were still everywhere and psychedelia was on the rise by the end of the year. Aimed at inducing the hallucinatory effects and intensified perceptions that LSD and other mind-expanding drugs produce, psychedelic prints were dream-like interpretations of a trip without the acid. The look was shiny and vibrant; surfaces reflected light, and colours were bright and saturated, from lime green to violet purple. Dresses made of paper debuted in the spring as the first intentionally disposable garments on the market (see Chapter 5). Synthetic materials were also being used in new, obvious ways – printed see-through and opaque vinyl raincoats and candy-coloured hard plastic jewelry made the most of the materials' qualities. The trend for fashion vinyl had originated with Paris designer Michèle Rosier the previous spring, but now vinyl boots, shoes, raincoats and umbrellas were being championed in the

US by Sylvia de Gay, one of the young designers recognized by a Coty Award for her contribution to youthful American fashions the previous autumn.

Paco Rabanne, who had been making handbags and accessories, debuted a small collection of dresses made of Rhodoid plastic discs in Paris in February 1966. 'The only new frontier left in fashion is the finding of new materials,' declared Rabanne, who then went on to experiment with chain mail and metal plaques linked with wire rings. Shown over naked models, his dresses revealed tantalizing glimpses of nudity through the gaps. However, those who purchased the dresses usually wore them over a body stocking. The chain-mail style inspired copies and adaptations, including chiffon gowns decorated with huge plastic sequins.

As hemlines rose on skirts, trousers became an appealing alternative for many women. Elegant palazzo styles remained popular for evenings, but for the young there were tighter-fitting trousers with flared legs for the discotheque. For daytime, young designers picked up on the idea of trouser suits for town wear. In New York it was Elite Jrs., a Seventh Avenue coat and suit house; the designer, Luba Roudenko Marks, created a beige gabardine suit consisting of straight trousers and a double-breasted military-style jacket featuring four flapped pockets with brass ball buttons. In Paris, it was

Opposite: Psychedelic animal-print silk dress by KEN SCOTT, Milan, *c*. 1966–67.

Right: Bead-and-sequin dress by HARRY ALGO, Paris, *c*. 1967–68.

Middle: Printed silk harem skirt evening dress by PUCCI, Florence, *c*. 1966.

Far right: Silk chiffon evening gown with large sequin paillettes decorating the halter top, OSCAR DE LA RENTA for JANE DERBY, New York, *c*. 1966–67.

Above: Dresses in leather and plastic sequins with metal chain-link seams by PACO RABANNE, Paris, *c.* 1966–68.

Right: Evening gown made of metal plaques and chain-link seams with ostrich-feather lining by PACO RABANNE, Paris, *c.* 1966–67.

Below and right: PACO RABANNE'S metal plaque dresses were first shown in Paris on nude models, but the cold metal dresses were more comfortable when worn over body stockings, *c.* 1966–68.

Yves Saint Laurent who was becoming known for his trousers; for spring 1966, white sailor trousers with a double-breasted navy jacket were especially well received.

In keeping with the move towards youthful, easy-moving clothes, underwear took on a more natural style. Courrèges and Gernreich had advocated going bra-less for over a year, and undergarments that controlled the figure were being dropped in favour of light, natural-looking brassieres and panties free of bones, wires, clips and control panels. Colourful prints made underwear look more like swimwear. Stockings and garters were also being displaced in favour of opaque and patterned tights, or sheer pantyhose, which had been on the US market since the beginning of the decade but were now preferred for wearing with shorter skirts. With the move towards less support and more bareness came a growing obsession with weight loss.

Jean Nidetch had founded Weight Watchers in America in May 1963, and in 1964 one of the first low-carbohydrate diets

Opposite left: Evening trouser suit in emerald and turquoise satin, SEKERS, Sloane Street, London, April 1966.

Opposite middle: Fringed trousers by JACQUES HEIM, Paris, March 1966.

Opposite right: Lace tights with built-in boots, and lace-and-chiffon top, CLAIRE HADDAD, Toronto, c. 1967.

Right: Trouser suit and cape by CASTILLO, Paris, autumn 1966.

Far right: Sailor-theme trousers and jacket by YVES SAINT LAURENT, Paris, spring 1966.

was advocated by Robert Cameron, author of *The Drinking Man's Diet*, in which he claimed that a steak washed down with a martini would yield weight loss. Diet foods were also appearing on the market, including Tab and Fresca – the one-calorie drinks from Coca-Cola – as well as the more nutritious meal-replacement drink Carnation Instant Breakfast. With smoking being the most common substitute for eating, the smoking rate was at its highest in history in the mid-to-late 1960s.

Fabrics also lost weight, and texture, in 1966; tweed and mohair were displaced by gabardine, poplin and jersey. Spring suits were unlined and apparently weightless, but dresses were rivalling suits for daytime wear. Simple sleeveless jersey designs were popular, but so were smock-style dresses with cuffed long sleeves and the body gathered into a yoke or collar that skimmed the figure. If not designed perfectly, daytime smock dresses could be mistaken for maternity wear, but for evening, sleeveless, airy chiffons hanging from jewelled collars looked elegant.

Spring news from Paris included shorter hems, trouser suits and tailored double-faced fabrics. Yves Saint Laurent offered the most excitement, including a surprisingly sporty nautical theme with bell-bottom trousers and striped T-shirts. Tent coats from Balenciaga in Paris and Norell in New York were well received and copied by other designers. For summer, baby-doll dresses were going strong in pale colours with lace trim, short skirts and flat shoes.

Trouser suits were in for every time of day and place for autumn. In New York, Luba's suits for Elite Jrs. were offered in camel-coloured gabardine with a collarless double-breasted jacket over straight trousers. For evening, there were trouser suits in purple or cherry-red velveteen, shown with foamy-lace blouses erupting from under the jacket at the throat and wrists. Yves Saint Laurent famously launched his elegant 'Le Smoking' trouser suit for women with the jacket cut like a man's tuxedo from another era. From Saint Laurent's black velvet

'Le Smoking' to yellow-beaded green silk pyjamas by Oscar de la Renta, the trouser suit was everywhere.

The spring trend for dresses in preference to suits strengthened as the year progressed, especially with the dress styles that obscured the figure, variously named 'smock', 'baby doll', 'cage', 'cocoon', 'shift', 'shirtdress' and 'chemise', available at every price level for every time of day. Yves Saint Laurent reasserted the Pop art dress with appliquéd designs in jersey, which he declared was 'the only modern material'. In a reverse of Warhol's Pop art classic Campbell's soup can appearing on a dress, American textile designer Ken Scott designed three styles of jersey dress to be sold in cans by the company Wippette.

Textured, patterned and tinted stockings were everywhere – in multicoloured fishnets or windowpane checks for day, and sparkly silver or gold at night. Shoes were lower-heeled than ever, and the newest look was for square toes. At the opposite end of the figure, hair was longer than before, achieved with the addition of a 'fall' hairpiece for length, and hairpieces at night for height. When combined with heavy eye make-up and big earrings, especially at night when earrings were huge, the look was disproportionately childlike.

On 28 November 1966, New York witnessed the party of the century, when author Truman Capote hosted a masked ball with 540 invitees that included a varied array of prominent personalities, from New York socialites to Hollywood actors. The event was the first and last of its kind, succeeding in being both elegant and irreverent at the same time, and mixing people of different ages and social backgrounds into one party. The masks concealed the identities of the couture-clad party-goers, who mingled freely with other guests and ate spaghetti at midnight. Cecil Beaton's horse-racing scene from the 1964 film *My Fair Lady* inspired the black-and-white theme, but instead of fantastic hats, masks were the focal point, ranging from 33-cent novelty-store masks to $600 feathered creations by Halston and Adolfo; these leading New York milliners

were transformed into dressmakers by the ball as they were commissioned to create gowns to compliment their elaborate masks. Sixteen-year-old Penelope Tree, who wore a dress from Paraphernalia by Betsey Johnson, was discovered by Diana Vreeland that evening, and went on to become a leading model and America's answer to Twiggy.

Most suits for spring 1967 from Paris and New York were either trouser suits or dresses with jackets. The waist was making a comeback in day dresses, with belts in chain, leather, suede or plastic reappearing. Norman Norell in New York showed the widest and most dramatic belt styles. Dresses without belts were often either indented at the waist, or fitted to a raised waistline and flowed out to the hem, which could be as short as five inches above the knee. Sleeves often matched this silhouette with skinny-fitting upper arms flowing out to bell bottoms at the wrists. The spring hit from Paris was Yves Saint Laurent's safari suit – a jacket with patch pockets that could be worn with skirts, shorts or trousers.

For evening, French and American designers favoured floaty, whirling-skirted gowns in bright or pastel-coloured silk jersey and chiffon trimmed with feathers, or petals and ruffles of silk chiffon. Alternatively, Paco Rabanne was enjoying the commotion his chain-mail and plastic-disc creations were stirring up, especially in the US where sales were brisk. For 'at home', casual evenings or summer patios, caftans were becoming strong sellers; they were extremely comfortable, and their pyramidal shape revealed little about the wearer's figure. They were offered in a range of artistic ethnic prints and embroideries, as well as bright floral or Modernist prints and swirling psychedelic patterns.

Some autumn 1967 Paris collections offered midi lengths. Measuring halfway between the knee and ankle, the midi met with mixed reactions. Some designers featured midi-length coats over miniskirts, and midi-length culottes or knickers looked especially good with knee-high boots. Marc Bohan for Dior had led the way for midi lengths, taking inspiration from

Below: Pop art copy of YVES SAINT LAURENT silhouette dress, Montreal c. 1966–67.

Left: A-line dresses by JEAN PATOU, Paris, spring 1967. Fuller hemlines and A-line shapes were in for this season.

Opposite top: Psychedelic-print chiffon evening chemises by PIERRE CARDIN, left, and TARONI, right, March 1967.

Opposite bottom: Tent coat by PIERRE CARDIN, Paris, spring 1967. The style had been introduced by BALENCIAGA the previous spring.

Opposite right: Orange-and-pink striped sleeveless shift by YOUTH GUILD, New York, c. 1966–67.

Above: Coat dress by EMANUEL UNGARO, Paris, spring 1967.

Left: Swiss chartreuse dress with jacket, labelled SCHIBLI MODELE, *c.* 1967.

Opposite left: The film *Doctor Zhivago* inspired MARC BOHAN for DIOR in autumn 1966.

Opposite middle: Jewelled short-sleeved shift with indented waist by MARC BOHAN for DIOR, Paris, autumn 1967.

Opposite right: NORMAN NORELL revives wide belts, full skirts and sleeves, autumn 1967.

the film *Doctor Zhivago*, which had been released in January 1966 to poor critical reviews. The film was a hit with the public and was still running in theatres when Marc Bohan showed Tsarist-inspired midi coats opulently trimmed with fox for his autumn 1966 collection. By autumn 1967, Nina Ricci was also going Russian, with wool coats and capes worn with black leather belts and fox trim. In New York, Chester Weinberg showed a brown velvet midi skirt edged in brown mink, with a lacy antique-style blouse. Nostalgia was becoming a strong influence, made stronger by the film *Bonnie and Clyde*, which inspired 1930s-style berets and patterned sweaters in some collections.

Fashion moved towards yet more historical references in late 1967 with a return to feminine ruffles, frills, lace and bows; there was more softness with suede, velvet and crêpe-back satin, and the colour black was back. Several New York collections featured mini-length black velvet evening dresses with antique lace trim, and miniskirts paired with high-collared lace blouses. For casual evening elegance Norell showed extremely wide belts with full skirts and full-sleeved tops for a buccaneer look. In Paris, medieval styling made an appearance, most acutely in the Balmain collection, which featured a long-sleeved white wool dress, shaped to the body, with a wide belt, long bell sleeves, jewel-tone beads and dark mink trim. Paris also showed evening dresses in airy black materials like gazar, with black, lacy stockings, and shoes with toes a little more rounded and heels a little higher than in previous seasons.

Italian fashions had displayed restrained enthusiasm for minis, but by 1967 Italian designers were adapting the look, developing a romantic elegance by relying upon rich textiles with curved seams, flared skirts and narrow waists. Several Italian designers had now achieved an equal status with the best French couturiers. New York stores carried both original

Right: Striped wool cape with leather helmet hat by PIERRE CARDIN, Paris, autumn 1967.

Far right: Canadian red-and-black leather cape with Italian black leather helmet hat labelled 'GIGI OF FLORENCE', *c.* 1966–67.

Opposite, top left: Midi coat over miniskirt by LANVIN, Paris, autumn 1967.

Opposite, bottom left: Midi coats by SCHERRER, autumn 1967.

Opposite, bottom right: VALENTINO trouser suit with maker's insignia, Rome, spring 1969.

Opposite, far right: Culottes by GUY LAROCHE, Paris, autumn 1967.

Italian fashions for autumn 1967, as well as licensed copies of Italian designs; Princess Galitzine had copies of her fashions at Lord & Taylor, while Fabiani had copies at Ohrbach's in New York. But none had more élan than Valentino, who had risen to become the hottest Italian designer of the year. He was still a couturier and would not venture into ready-to-wear until the 1970s, although he was now dabbling with lines of raincoats and menswear, as well as creating a scent. Valentino took to using 'V' as his signature motif in textiles and findings, like Chanel's interlocked double 'C's and Pucci's signature-print silk jersey.

Other designers were also picking up on the idea of branding their designs with their names or insignia, including Chester Weinberg, Barocco, B. H. Wragge, Adolfo, Rudi Gernreich and Elio Berhanyer. Fifty years earlier, it had been the practice for fashionable ladies to keep the names of their dressmakers secret, but the rise of ready-to-wear brought cachet to the wearer of a desirable designer's garment or accessory when it brandished a recognizable cipher. Bill Blass commented in an article in *Life* on 13 June 1969, 'It's a curious thing that women who would consider it vulgar and ostentatious to wear their own initials or crest run around in designers' initials or names.'

WHO WILL
DO LAUNDRY
IN SPACE?

LOOKING TO
THE FUTURE

'In the self-consciously modern mid-1960s, the quest for a space-age future had created a progress-minded society ready to embrace the ephemeral quality of disposable paper apparel.'

In 1950, man-made materials (including rayon) made up only 15 per cent of the textile market; this figure would rise to 50 per cent by 1970. As synthetics such as nylon, Corfam, Orlon, Terylene, Lurex and spandex were introduced to the market, manufacturers would promote each new material, praising its qualities: wrinkle-free and stain-resistant, colour-fast, cheaper to maintain and able to hold permanent pleats! Some of the most successful textiles resulted from blends of natural fibres with synthetics that brought out the best qualities of both. Many of the new textiles were promoted through full-page fashion magazine advertisements that featured a garment by a well-known designer, showcasing the material's attributes.

Not all new materials were successful. Corfam, for example, was the first of the faux leathers to debut; DuPont exhibited the wonder leather at its 1964 New York World's Fair pavilion. Its advantages were breathability, durability and a perma-polish finish that required nothing more than a damp cloth to clean it.

However, its primary disadvantage was a stiffness that never lessened with wear. DuPont spent millions of dollars developing, making and marketing Corfam, but the product never caught on and was later abandoned as a substitute for shoe leather in 1971. The synthetics market experienced an overall decline when the oil crisis of 1973 caused a surge in the price of petrochemicals used to make most of the materials.

One of the more unusual offerings brought forth in the 'anything new is good' optimism of the 1960s was paper yardage reinforced with rayon or nylon scrim. The American paper companies Scott and Kimberly-Stevens began making this durable paper and test-marketing its commercial potential. Scott used a rayon mesh scrim for Dura-weave, while Kimberly-Stevens used a nylon mesh scrim for Kaycel, for which it followed the tradition of using names beginning with the letter 'K' for its products, as it had done with Kleenex facial tissues and Kotex feminine hygiene products.

Page 108: Raquel Welch wearing futuristic plastic fashions, 1967.

Right: White paper ballgown created by WALTER HOLMES to showcase the material's potential, September 1965.

Above and right: The two original
designs offered by SCOTT PAPER,
with a Canadian magazine order
form and promotional image,
summer 1966.

Both Scott and Kimberly-Stevens saw potential for industrial and institutional paper clothing and textiles, but were concerned about how to market the material – they didn't want to overstate its qualities or underrate its possibilities. Thinking the product might be rejected for lack of durability if it was called paper, Kimberly-Stevens referred to Kaycel as a 'disposable' or 'non-woven' product in all promotional materials. Some encouraging feedback was received from test sites at hospitals in Michigan and California that were comparing the cost efficiency of the old washable and the new disposable types of bedding and garments: disposable was easier to use, but laundering was still cheaper.

In 1965, Robert Bayer, an engineer working with Scott Paper, felt there might be commercial potential in paper fashion. He asked his wife to design a simple A-line dress pattern for making up garments to sell to department stores as a novelty beach cover-up or summer frock. No interest could be stirred, however, so Scott made the dress as a promotional item. As a sponsor of the televised Junior Miss Pageant in 1966, Scott previewed its dresses on the nationwide broadcast and then launched sales in April across the US; a Canadian launch followed in August. For $1.25, one of two paper dresses could be ordered through the mail – a red-and-yellow bandana print, or a black-and-white Op art print – sold under the label Paper Caper.

Every dress came with a slip of paper that explained how to alter and care for the dress as well as a warning that washing would remove fire retardants: 'To shorten the paper dress, all that is needed is a steady hand and a pair of scissors. To mend it, sticky tape is dandy.... While you should not count on more than one wearing, depending on use many have been able to get three or four wearings from a Paper Caper dress. You can also cut up the dress for using as disposable guest towels, placemats or an apron... It will never displace that little black dress as a wardrobe staple, but as a conversation piece, as an attention attraction, the Paper Caper is unique.'

By year's end, despite having sold nearly half a million dresses, Scott had made little profit from direct sales, as they had sold the products at near cost. However, upon hearing of the success of the Scott dresses, the media jumped on the story and a flood of commentary appeared. Despite the positive publicity that surpassed Scott's marketing strategy, the company had no intentions of continuing the paper dress venture into 1967.

Following on the heels of the Scott paper-dress launch, Kimberly-Stevens was contracted by the North Carolina hosiery manufacturer Mars of Asheville to supply Kaycel for a paper-dress venture that was purely a fashion enterprise. The new line was launched under the label Waste Basket Boutique and hit the market in June 1966.

When the *New York Times* reported on 6 September 1966 that paper fabric shifts were appearing on the streets of New York, paper dresses gained credibility – if they were being worn in New York, they must be fashion! The most avid industry representative of paper-dress futures was Ronald Bard, vice-president of Mars of Asheville. Bard was quoted in that same article, saying, 'Five years from now 75 per cent of the nation will be wearing disposable clothing.' At the time it looked like he might be right. By the end of the year, Mars of Asheville was the leading manufacturer in disposables, producing 80,000 paper garments per week; 1.4 million had been sold and sales amounted to $3.5 million. Mars of Asheville's projected revenue for 1967 topped $6 million, but halfway through the year those projections were reconfigured to be closer to $30 million.

In the self-consciously modern mid-1960s, the quest for a space-age future had created a progress-minded society ready to embrace the ephemeral quality of disposable paper apparel. The *Seattle Post-Intelligencer* had reported back at the beginning of the fad on 14 June 1966, 'Wear the shift and then toss it away. No washing helps take care of water shortage.' Julian Tomshin, a textile designer who became fascinated with the paper apparel phenomenon, was quoted in the 25 November

Right: Dress and premium offer for *Yellow Pages* print, 1968.

Below left: Promotional *Time* magazine dress, 1967.

Below middle: Universal Studios' 'The Big Ones of '68' promotional paper dress featuring silk-screen portraits of leading actors and actresses and the films they appeared in during the year.

Below right: Promotional Campbell's 'Souper' dress, spring 1967.

Opposite: Premium offer for paper dresses from Breck Shampoo.

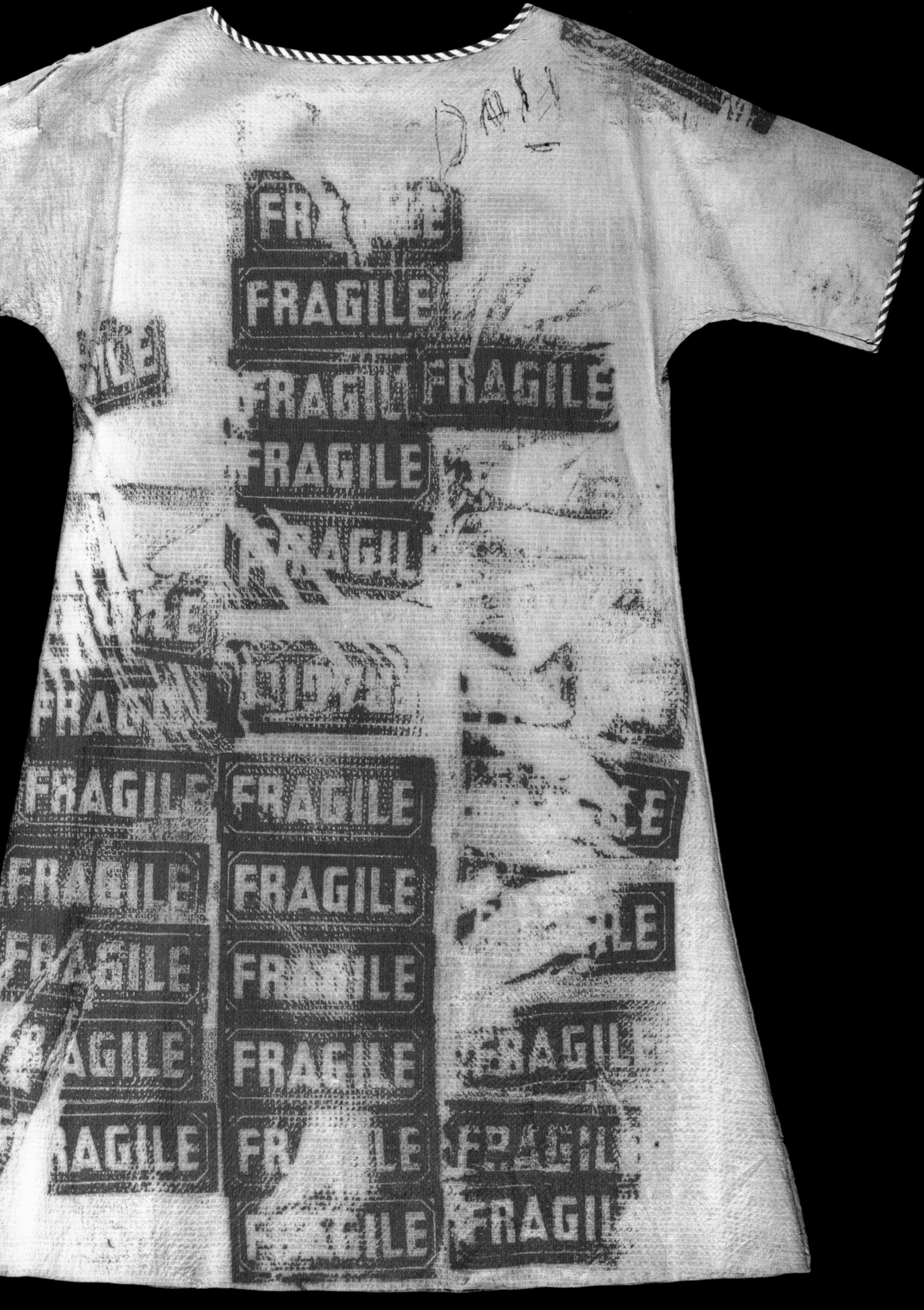

FRAGILE
FRAGILE
FRAGILE
FRAGILE
FRAGILE
FRAGILE
FRAGILE
FRAGILE
FRAGILE

1966 issue of *Life* as saying, 'It's right for our age, after all who is going to do laundry in space?' Tomshin believed that improved techniques would bring prices down until garments would be packaged in tear-off rolls, like sandwich bags, and sold in vending machines.

However, established fashion retailers were less enthusiastic about the future of paper clothing. Most industry authorities were quoted as being open to the idea that it was a great gag for summer fun, but would never overtake the tradition of silk or wool clothing. The *Financial Post* reported on 17 September 1966, 'Where they can compete economically consumers will buy paper garments that retail less than the cost of laundering or dry cleaning cloth garments, or offer greater convenience by being disposable.'

The Wadsworth Atheneum museum in Hartford, Connecticut, had held a famous paper ball in 1936, and in late 1966 decided it was time to host another paper party. Fashion journalist and society commentator Marilyn Bender wrote in *The Beautiful People*, 'No need to worry that such a democratic dress – one that absolutely anyone can afford – will destroy the fashion elite. The woman of wealth and social contacts can commission an artist to create a special paper dress for a special event, then donate it to a museum, provided the garment hasn't deteriorated on the dance floor.' As Bender predicted, instead of cheap and cheerful disposable paper frocks, designers were hired to create unique couture creations for the event. Three examples of hand-painted gowns by New York textile designer Tzaims Luksus cost $1,000 each and were featured in the 25

Opposite: When paint-it-yourself dress kits were introduced onto the market in spring 1967, the Brooklyn department store Abraham & Straus commissioned Andy Warhol to paint a dress during an in-store 'happening'. Warhol stencilled 'fragile' into a dress while it was being worn by a model, and then signed the dress 'Dali'. The dress was later donated to the Brooklyn Museum of Art by the store.

Right: Dress and premium offer from Jolly Green Giant vegetable company, *c.* 1967.

November issue of *Life* magazine. The dresses became part of the Wadsworth's permanent collection.

In an attempt to bring a serious respectability to the fad, *Look* magazine commissioned the photographer Horst P. Horst to shoot a series of paper dresses by leading designers, including a gold foil paper evening gown by Fabiani, black-and-white print culottes by Pucci, a wedding dress by Belville, a short white dress by Dior and a quilted silver evening coat by Givenchy that looked more like a breakfast coat. Horst himself even designed a green paper suit that was modelled by Steve McQueen for the December 1966 photoshoot. The images were published in the 7 March 1967 issue of *Look* magazine, but while the clothes had big names behind their designs, the fashions were not particularly imaginative. During 1967,

many designers from Mr. Blackwell to Paco Rabanne created paper dresses, and in early 1968 Bonnie Cashin planned a line of clothes called Paper-Route, but the paper-clothing fad was fading by then and it doesn't appear that Cashin's line went into production.

Lesser-known designers seemed to have better ideas on how to make saleable paper-clothing styles. New York-based Elisa Daggs had come from a background of fashion editing for *Harper's Bazaar*, *Vogue*, *Charm* and *Brides* magazines. In 1967 she created several paper garments that were picked up by department stores including Bonwit Teller and Lord & Taylor. Daggs's kimono-style geometric-cut garments suited the stiff material, however, her striped kaftans and waterproof paper raincoats were not intended for those who liked cheap

Above: Designer paper dresses photographed by Horst P. Horst for *Look* magazine, December 1966: gold foil dress by FABIANI and quilted silver dress by GIVENCHY. Steve McQueen wears a green paper suit designed by Horst.

Left: Gold foil dress with ruffled collar, designed for the TWA French service by ELISA DAGGS, 1968.

Opposite left and middle: MEXI MIA disposables, autumn 1966.

Opposite right: Robe with tie belt, designed for the TWA Italian service by ELISA DAGGS, 1968.

Right and above: Reemay dresses, *c.* 1967–68, and artist's drawings of the dresses, used in the packaging.

clothing. In 1967 Daggs was commissioned to design a paper sari to be used as a promotional item for Air India, and in 1968 she created four stewardess dresses for Trans World Airlines (TWA) flights from New York to Los Angeles, London, Paris and Rome, all of which were also available for purchase at airport gift shops and select stores. Daggs's clothes were chic and desirable to those at the top end of the market. The *Seattle Post-Intelligencer* quoted her in an article on 25 May 1967: 'Let's get one thing straight right away – a disposable dress is a luxury. It is not for the poor. Only people with money can afford to buy things to use a few times and throw away.... Much of the new paper material is fireproof but then it can't be cleaned or washed. There is no use trying to approach this from a practical standpoint. You have to have fun with it, in a riot of color. I think my place is that I have added the fashion element. I haven't gooked the clothes up with buttons or zippers. They all work as simply as an envelope. They wrap, tie, and they are all made in one size with expandable sides or back.... Paper clothes won't die. Just by the nature of the material, they create a new fashion architecture but until they can be made by fusing or molding instead of being cut and sewn – five or six years from now, maybe – there is no point at all in treating them as anything but what they are: expensive fun.'

Judith Brewer, a California designer with a boutique in Beverly Hills, was also raising the fashion level of the disposable dress, along with its price. Her dresses sold for between $10 and $40, with a top-end price of $200 for a paper fur coat.

In October 1966, Moda Mia, a division of the cosmetics combine Rayette-Fabergé Inc., launched their line of Mexican-print shifts, Mexi Mia, that sold for $1.98 in drug stores and supermarkets. The dresses were made of Fibron, a disposable rayon mesh fabric that had tiny perforations over the entire surface. Fibron was made by Chicopee Mills and was introduced in the 1950s as a limited-use kitchen cleaning cloth that could be washed several times before discarding. The cloths were marketed under the brand name Handi-wipes in the US and J-Cloth in Canada and the UK. Moda Mia's launch of Fibron may have seemed like a foray into a new alternative disposable material, but in reality it was a response to a growing shortage of paper.

Scott was now focusing on industrial uses for its Dura-weave and Kimberly-Stevens already had agreements with buyers, primarily Mars of Asheville, for most of their Kaycel, leaving little surplus to sell anywhere else. In an article in Toronto's *Financial Post* on 8 April 1967, Canadian manufacturers complained that no mill in Canada was making Kaycel and they had to rely on imports from the US. Montreal's Louben Sportswear, the only Canadian manufacturer of disposable dresses, had managed to secure enough Kaycel from Kimberly-Stevens, but other Canadian manufacturers had to do without. *Parade* magazine reported in its 18 June 1967 issue that Ron Bard, vice-president of Mars of Asheville, had admitted that 'about 75 per cent of the major department stores carry our line. I've had to turn down premium offers from abroad because of supply problems.' Kimberly-Stevens had a backlog of orders for Kaycel running into late autumn. Its machines were so busy the firm began planning a new plant to manufacture paper textiles only. *Time* magazine had quipped on 17 March 1967 that all customers of Kaycel were now on 'K-rations.... Manufacturers are turning to Dupont's Reemay® as an alternative.'

Reemay was a textile made from polyester filaments bonded into position by heat and pressure. Unlike paper, Reemay needed no reinforcing scrim to keep it from tearing, it was machine washable up to a half dozen times, lightweight, strong, drape-able, resisted wrinkling and had an attractive surface with a subtle swirl pattern that showed through the print design. First produced in 1964, Reemay was originally intended as an interlining material.

Dupont had also developed Tyvek from high-density thermoplastic polyolefin fibres. These two products had outstanding toughness and puncture resistance, but no porosity. Mars of Asheville had employed Tyvek in creating disposable swimming trunks in 1966, sold primarily to hotels and motels that provided them to guests who had forgotten to pack a swimsuit. Unfortunately, the trunks trapped air, which embarrassingly bubbled up from under the water's surface. Despite this issue, 3,000 suits were sold within the first year.

By summer 1967 more manufacturers were turning to Reemay, Fibron and Tyvek to produce their disposable clothing. The market was now more accurately described as disposable rather than paper, since alternative materials had filled the void left by the short supply of Dura-weave and Kaycel.

Although men were less enthusiastic about paper clothing, Mars of Asheville, James Sterling and Day's Sportswear test-marketed men's paper trousers and suits in the spring of 1967. The American artist James Rosenquist also made a stir at his Pop art openings by wearing a custom-made brown paper suit. However, the manufacturing techniques needed to replicate the traditional tailoring of slacks and jackets made the suits unprofitable, and the men's paper-clothing market never caught on.

Twisted paper for use as yarn in making women's hats and handbags showed up in craft stores, as manufacturers attempted to widen the market. Butterick, McCall and Vogue printed patterns specifically for paper garments. Designs were free-form so they needed no facings, armholes were cut deeper to avoid tearing, and neck and sleeve edges were stitched by machine.

The Canadian pulp and paper industry showcased paper's possibilities in its pavilion at Expo 67 in Montreal. Clothes for men and women, shoes, bedspreads, chairs, lamps – the variations were endless. Stores like Paperworks in Manhattan offered paper curtains, drapes and sheets, as well as cardboard furniture. In the summer of 1967 a 'Design-in' was organized in New York's Central Park. Participants sat on paper chairs and saw the official launch of the 'Plydom', a 375-square-foot paper house designed by Howard Yates that could be set up in two hours. Designed as a vacation property, the aluminium frame and accordion-pleated laminated-paper home

had already been test-marketed in California as housing for migrant workers. The laminating process was a breakthrough for the future of paper, and the 'Plydom' was touted as a model for what someday might become lunar housing.

Combining Pop art with paper dresses, Harry Gordon, an American graphic artist living in England, produced some of the most successful designs of the disposable trend. He produced six dresses in 1967 with photo images of a cat, eye, rose, rocket ship, a hand in the Buddhist gesture of peace with a poem by Allen Ginsberg on the palm, and Bob Dylan. The dresses were sold through Harrods and various boutiques in London, as well as in Le Drugstore in Paris. For its American release in spring 1968, Bob Dylan was dropped from the series because 'Dylan didn't like being worn', according to a 3 March 1968 article in the *Winnipeg Free Press*. Plans for a full-colour second series for autumn 1968 were never put into production because the paper-dress fad had faded by the end of the year.

Mildred Custin, president of Bonwit Teller in New York, was quoted in the *New York Times* at the height of the paper-dress fad on 21 February 1967: 'The demand has surprised us but I see it on a long term basis as more important in the industrial and utility field than in the fashion area…it will have a life for at least several seasons in specialized apparel categories but it may turn out to be just a fad.' Custin's prediction was very accurate.

Many women who tried paper and disposable dresses found them less than satisfactory. Although the garments were never intended for more than one wearing there seemed to be disappointment upon discovering this to be true. The dresses billowed when the wearer sat, and sleeved styles would often bind. Hems had a tendency to bend and crease along the edge, called 'crocking'. Paper also suggested easy access, like gift wrap on a parcel, and many women experienced undue attention while wearing a paper dress to a party.

Despite their meteoric success as a promotional tool, the coupon offers in magazines for paper dresses dwindled, and articles on the subject slowly disappeared throughout 1968.

The Canadian magazine *Chatelaine* reported in February 1968: 'In the future, when our homes become dust-free and housework automated, white clothes will be practical – disposable or not. In future, materials that change colour to match surroundings, adjust to temperature changes, too, may be available. Plastic may one day be extruded into flexible shapes for all types of clothes.'

By 1969, the hippie movement's back-to-nature awareness and growing anti-pollution message was beginning to change public perceptions of a disposable society. What had been associated with futurism was now seen as wasteful. However, as Scott and Kimberly-Stevens had publicly stated in 1966, a lasting business for disposable apparel did remain in industrial and institutional applications, for which the paper yardage had originally been developed.

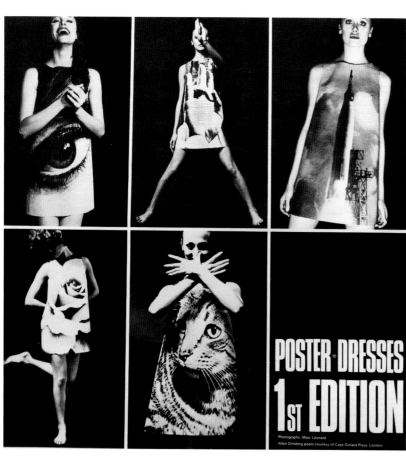

Above: Poster dresses by HARRY GORDON released for the North American market in spring 1968.

Above right: Paper dresses by HARRY GORDON, 1967–68.

Previous page: Paper earrings set – one of the many possibilities for the material, *c.* 1967–68.

Right: Bob Dylan poster dress by HARRY GORDON, 1967. The initial release in the UK included Dylan, but the dress was removed before the American release in spring 1968.

Political campaigning in 1968 took advantage of the paper-dress billboard. Designs promoted Richard Nixon, George W. Romney and Robert F. Kennedy.

ROMNEY FOR PRESIDENT

NIXON

DOING YOUR OWN THING: THE RISE OF NON-CONFORMISM

'I really don't give a damn about clothes.... Basically clothes are a façade, nothing more. I groove on my clothes now because I have to.'

Janis Joplin, 1968, quoted in *Rags*, 1970

By the end of 1966, Beatle boots, 'poor-boy' sweaters and vinyl miniskirts were available at most department stores throughout Europe and North America. Boutiques were looking for the next trend and that inspiration came from the past. Before the word 'vintage' was applied to the field of buying and selling old garments, one of the first and most famous used-clothing ventures in London was I Was Lord Kitchener's Valet, an antiques shop in Portobello Road that also carried Victorian dresses and decommissioned military uniforms. Robert Orbach, the store manager, recalled in a 2006 interview with the Victoria and Albert Museum, 'Mick Jagger bought a red Grenadier guardsman drummer's jacket...and wore it on *Ready Steady Go!*...performing "Paint it Black" [on 27 May 1966]. The next morning there was a line of about 100 people wanting to buy the tunic...and we sold everything in the shop by lunchtime.' By summer some mod men, and even women, were strolling the streets in Victorian military and livery jackets. Not all wartime veterans appreciated the carefree wearing of military uniforms for fashion, but as the manager of the Portobello Road shop explained to *The Times* in September 1966, 'Our uniforms are all bought and sold legally and they are all obsolete so why shouldn't they be worn?' The shop became so successful that more branches were opened, and it even became the topic of a song by Peter Fenton:

I was Lord Kitchener's valet,
We were ever so pally:
I was always there to press his suits
And clean his boots
And in return as everybody knows,
He gave me all his old clothes.

I was Lord Kitchener's valet,
We used to share the same chalet.
He would often say that when he died
That he'd provide for me,

And you can see just what I got:
His winter woollies and the lot.
Oh Lord Kitchener, what a to-do,
Everyone is wearing clothes that once belonged to you.
If you were alive today I'm sure you would explode,
If you took a stroll down the Portobello Road.

I was Lord Kitchener's valet,
Right from Panama to Calais,
I was by his side to wipe his shoes
And serve his booze
I knew my loyalty would be repaid:
I'm in the second-hand trade.

Oh Lord Kitchener, what a to-do,
Everyone is wearing clothes that once belonged to you.
I know that you'll forgive me if I tell you on my knees:
Your wardrobe is a victim of the economic squeeze.

The boutique Granny Takes a Trip opened on King's Road in early 1966 in an area referred to as World's End – the undesirable stretch at the opposite end from Sloane Square where the high-class shops were located. Granny Takes a Trip opened as an antique clothing store, but the stock sold too quickly and modern pieces, heavily inspired by the past, were introduced: frilly shirts, brocade vests and satin scarves were made to keep the racks filled. Bolstering this fashion flashback was an exhibition of Aubrey Beardsley's work at the Victoria and Albert Museum during the summer of 1966 that further inspired the nostalgia for turn-of-the-century style. The first shop sign for Granny Takes a Trip was painted in red Art Nouveau lettering on a black background, picking up on the heirloom mood of the merchandise within. Nigel Waymouth, owner of Granny Takes a Trip, recalled in an interview in Dominic Sandbrook's *White Heat*, 'The shop definitely had an intimidating quality, a mystique…. It was full of a cluttered jumble of Victorian bustles, Boer War helmets, Ottoman fezzes, Charleston dresses and

Chicago gangster suits, alongside photos of Edwardian chorus girls, antique swords, glass walking sticks, Victorian feather boas and an early gramophone. A catch-all assemblage of dash and dandyism through the ages.' The same month Granny Takes a Trip opened, an event at the Marquee Club on Wardour Street in Soho specified on its invitation: 'Costume, masque, ethnic, space, Edwardian, Victorian, and hipness generally… face and body make-up – certainly.' The trend for vintage was so strong in London that *Life* commented in its 2 December 1966 issue: '…in mod and mini London, the style kick is suddenly old clothes. English youth is deserting Carnaby Street in favor of Portobello Road, which is no fashion centre but a flea market of some 20 years standing…. The mania for old clothes springs from this happy combination of stylish good looks and economy. Shoppers delight in prowling not just Portobello Road but Chelsea as well for attic-rescued finery that has nostalgic elegance and contemporary punch. High on the list of such discoveries are lavishly beaded evening dresses of the 20s and 30s and Victorian nightgowns – now sold not just as sleepwear but also as party dresses.'

Arriving in London in late September 1966, American musician Jimi Hendrix picked up on the vintage dandy look and was soon frequenting Carnaby Street for velvet suits and flared hipster trousers, as well as Portobello for antique military jackets. He acquired a Hussar's black wool jacket trimmed with gold tasselled ropes, and a Royal Veterinary Corps dress jacket in scarlet red wool; a group of policemen reportedly once ordered him to remove it because they considered wearing it an offence to the memory of the original owner. Hendrix's style became a distinct mix of mod and antique dandy clothing. When he returned to the US in June 1967, appearing at the Monterey International Pop Music Festival in California, he wore a hand-painted silk jacket by Chris Jagger (Mick's brother) and a bright pink feather boa, but he also wore his antique military jackets for other performances around the same time – along with a variety of psychedelic patterned

Page 127: I Was Lord Kitchener's Valet boutique, London, early 1967.

Left: Jimi Hendrix at a performance in Ann Arbor, Michigan, 15 August 1967.

shirts and scarves, ethnic embroidered silk jackets and vests, and plenty of jewelry: rings, necklaces and medallions.

The old clothing trend received more press coverage in the UK, but it was as strong in America, especially on the West Coast. Yves Saint Laurent's military look for autumn 1966 inspired more American women to try vintage shopping, according to *Life*, which said on 30 September that 'the fad for military outfits has taken hold in the US where young girls are digging through second-hand shops for authentic uniforms... which they call "soul clothes" because they are the genuine article.' However, not everyone understood the fashion. California designer James Galanos commented on how baffled he was by the idea of wearing someone else's old clothes.

The American trend dates back to June 1965, when the Red Dog Saloon opened for business in Virginia City, an old mining town near Reno, Nevada, where Mark Twain had started his writing career in the 1860s. The bar owner hired an unknown folk-rock band called The Charlatans, primarily because of the way they dressed – in cowboy boots, vests and straw boaters, for a uniquely old-fashioned American look that could not be mistaken for British mod. During the summer, the band's fans began dressing up like gunslingers and saloon girls; the fashion followed the group to San Francisco, where they played for the first time on 30 August 1965. The Charlatans became known for their western vintage look assembled from used clothing and thrift shops, and furthered the trend just as the music scene was exploding in the city.

There were differences between what the British and Americans wore, and how they wore it. In London, vintage clothes were an extension of mod dandyism and granny chic, but in the US vintage was transformed by the hippie movement into more of an expression of rebellion against conformity and affluence. The wearing of Victorian scarlet military tunics carried no political message in the UK, but in the US a khaki army surplus jacket worn with a flower in a buttonhole silently protested the war in Vietnam. Writer Dell Franklin recalled

in Barry Miles's *Hippie* that upon his arrival in San Francisco in May 1967, 'When I spotted kids wearing army surplus field jackets patched with peace symbols and North Vietnam flags, I left my own well-worn field jacket, the only remnant of my military wardrobe, in...the Chevy station wagon....'

Even before hippies were defined as a social movement, non-conformity had been well established in music and fashion by American youth idols such as Bob Dylan and Sonny & Cher. 'Now what do they care about the clothes I wear?' was a line from a 1965 Sonny Bono song, inspired by an incident during which he had been asked to leave a café because of the way he was dressed. In a *Life* article from November 1965 it was revealed that Cher didn't own a dress, nor Sonny a tie: 'Our clothes are consistent with our personalities,' said Sonny. The two were known for bucking dress codes and wearing heavy Neanderthal-looking bobcat fur vests to formal dinner parties; Cher's trademark look included snugly fitted hipster slacks with flared bell-bottom legs. *Life* noted, 'She has hundreds of them, every color but black, brown or grey, and thousands of her fans who regard her as a style-setter have taken to wearing them too.'

In the early 1960s, the folk music scene centred in New York's Greenwich Village was a hub of political activism, but no distinct fashion evolved to accompany the protest songs. In fact fashion in New York remained notably staid and respectable, avoiding any suggestion of radical subversion. San Francisco, however, was also a centre of cultural dissent in post-war America, especially for fashion, and it was here that beat bohemianism was visually transformed into the hippie generation.

American hippies were almost entirely white, middle-class kids rebelling against the anxieties of their parents' generation, following the ideals of peace, love, collective ownership and the right to do your own thing. Hippies read the works of Thoreau and Gandhi, tuned in to the spiritual philosophies of Buddha and Krishna, embraced naturalism, protested against war, promoted civil rights, practised yoga, ate organic food, celebrated free love, joined environmental groups, took drugs, and dressed to express anti-materialism and self-enlightenment.

Marijuana use had been rampant among the beats and remained popular with hippies, but it was the hallucinogenic drug lysergic acid diethylamide (LSD), which could be legally procured in the US between 1963 and 1966, that became particularly associated with the movement. LSD distorted reality and heightened perceptions and senses, and became the impetus for the creation of psychedelic art and music.

Weekly concerts at various venues in San Francisco starting in late 1965 started to include 'liquid light shows' – film projections and light effects that enhanced the performances of psychedelic rock bands like the Grateful Dead and Jefferson Airplane. Up-and-coming local acts used clothing to create their image; designer Jeanne Rose made a shirt for a musician

in 1965 and was soon getting calls from other bands. In short order Jeanne had a business creating stage garments for Big Brother and the Holding Company, Jefferson Airplane and the Young Rascals. She became known as a designer of comfortable clothing made from plush materials that felt natural while performing, especially while high. Fellow designer Linda Gravenites worked mostly as a theatre costumer before she began making clothes for Janis Joplin in 1967. She suggested Joplin should go for a 'chick pirate' look, wrapped in finery. Gravenites spent the next two years creating trouser suits from lace tablecloths, purses refashioned from 1920s beaded dresses, tie-dye velvet blouses and ponchos cut from Victorian fringed piano shawls.

Bands congregated in the Haight-Ashbury area of San Francisco where apartments in Victorian homes were spacious

Far left: Sonny & Cher, while on tour in the UK, July 1965.

Left: A couple in San Francisco's Golden Gate Park, August 1967.

Opposite left: Indian embroidered shirt, c. 1967–68

Opposite right: Hippies dancing in a field in Los Angeles, summer 1967.

Page 135: 'Flower People' wedding, Oslo, c. 1967.

and cheap. Other like-minded artists followed, and by the autumn of 1966 art happenings, vegetarian restaurants and theatre troupes had developed the neighbourhood into 'Hashbury', a thriving hippie community that had its own dress code and media. Counter-culture newspapers like the *Berkeley Barb* and *Rolling Stone* spread the hippie gospel, and there was even a fashion magazine from the same editorial office as *Rolling Stone*, called *Rags*, briefly published late in the movement, from June 1970 to June 1971. San Francisco's Haight Street never had the fashion sense of London's King's Road, where hippie style was an artful blend of real and inspired vintage and ethnic colourfully patterned garments and accessories. American hippie fashion tended to be less coordinated and intentionally shabby, but the motivation behind it was predominantly political at first, rather than artistic.

Although 'hippiness' was spreading well beyond America's borders during 1966, most Americans were still not familiar with what or who a hippie was. That began to change on 6 October 1966 when the Love Pageant Rally took place in San Francisco's Golden Gate Park to protest the criminalization of LSD. As confrontations between police and hippies had been escalating, a non-confrontational approach was urged by organizers who hoped to turn the protest into more of a festival. Posters advertising the event requested participants to bring 'the color gold...photos of personal saints and gurus and heroes of the underground...children...flowers... flutes...drums...feathers...bands...beads...banners...flags... incense...chimes...gongs...cymbals...symbols...costumes.'

The Monterey Pop Festival in June 1967 initiated the start of what became known as the 'Summer of Love'. Up to 100,000

youths descended upon the city that summer, guided by Scott McKenzie's song 'San Francisco', in which he exhorted them to wear flowers in their hair – and many did just that, earning themselves the name 'flower children'.

On 7 July 1967 *Time* printed a feature on the hippie scene: 'Hippies preach altruism and mysticism, honesty, joy and non-violence. They find an almost childish fascination in beads, blossoms and bells, blinding strobe lights and ear-shattering music, exotic clothing and erotic slogans. Their professed aim is nothing less than the subversion of Western society by "flower power" and force of example… Last week the sidewalks and doorways were filling with new arrivals – hippies and would-be hippies with suitcases and sleeping bags, just off the bus and looking for a place to "crash" (sleep). Wise hippies wrap themselves in serapes against the San Francisco chill, or else wear old army or navy foul-weather jackets and sturdy boots. One way to identify the new arrivals is by their mod clothes: carefully tailored corduroy pants, hip-snug military jackets, snap-brimmed hats like those worn by Australian soldiers.'

Tourists and rubberneckers in search of psychedelic poster shops, bangle bracelet boutiques and a glimpse of public nudity became a part of the Hashbury scene on weekends. However, what had started as a celebration of love, peace and tolerance spiralled into social chaos; the city was unprepared to accommodate the massive influx of youths who didn't get the true meaning of the movement and came to San Francisco primarily for drugs and sex. In *Hippie*, Barry Miles recounted an impromptu visit to San Francisco on 7 August by George Harrison and his then wife, Pattie Boyd. As George and Pattie strolled the streets of Hashbury they were gradually recognized and a crowd began to follow; someone pushed a guitar into George's hand, but George had taken a hit of acid and couldn't remember the words of any songs, so he handed the guitar back and the crowd began to boo. Harrison recalled, 'I thought it would be something like King's Road only more. Somehow I expected them all to own their own little shops. I expected them all to be nice and clean and friendly and happy…. They were all terribly dirty and scruffy…hideous, spotty little teenagers.'

For the real hippies of San Francisco, the Summer of Love had been a disappointing period of drug abuse and panhandling. Tired of the gawkers, journalists and runaway kids from back east, the Diggers, a street theatre troupe who are credited with originating the phrases 'Do your own thing' and 'Today is the first day of the rest of your life', ceremoniously ended the Summer of Love on 6 October, the first anniversary of the criminalization of LSD, with a mock funeral for the 'death of the hippie'.

In case any middle-class readers in suburban America were still unfamiliar with what hippies were, the January 1968 edition of *Look* featured images by Irving Penn of hippies adorned in beads, flowers and bells. The article also featured images of the Hell's Angels – the leather-clad motorcycle club that had become associated with leading figures of the hippie counter-culture.

While mod had been about consumerism and conformity, the hippie movement was about the cause; fashion wasn't supposed to look like it mattered, and yet it became the source of a dominant trend. The unkempt, hirsute look, as celebrated by the rock musical *Hair*, which opened for a four-year run on Broadway in April 1968, became a leading style for young American men. 'Get a haircut!' was a commonly heard epithet from those who saw long-haired hippies as un-American. Eugene McCarthy's presidential campaign in 1968 asked young Democrat canvassers to 'get clean for Gene' by shaving beards and cutting hair to meet middle-class expectations.

Hippie culture was now changing and splitting into more factions with different priorities and interests: there were back-to-the-land communes, political dissidents and activists, new religion followers and psychedelic music fans. American hippie fashion diverged between an adoption of jeans as a kind of young, rebellious working-class uniform, and a more artistic fashion sense that blended ethnic, vintage and hand-crafted garments and accessories. Boutiques catering to the growing interest for

Above left: Embroidered orange-
and-purple rayon-velvet trouser suit,
made in India for export, late 1960s.

Above right: Printed cotton robe
with appliquéd mirrorwork, made
in Pakistan for export, late 1960s.

Right: Woven tunic, labelled
'NEW GENERATION – made in
England', *c.* 1967–69. With
Moroccan saddle-bag purse and
peace symbol necklace, late 1960s.

Above: Janis Joplin at the Chelsea Hotel, New York, 3 March 1969.

Left: Blue-thread-embroidered suede coat with goat-fur trim and lining, made in Afghanistan for export, *c.* 1968–73.

BEAUTIFY AMERICA get a haircut

exotic fashions imported items from anywhere with a psychedelic aesthetic: Moroccan dashikis, Mexican floral embroidered shifts and Indian kurtas. Afghani goatskin vests and coats with paisley silk embroidery and shaggy white fur lining were especially popular after John Lennon famously wore one in May 1967 at the launch of the album *Sgt. Pepper's Lonely Hearts Club Band*. Exotic and antique textiles including Indian saris, Indonesian batiks and grandma's linens were sold as yardage to tent rooms or transformed into shifts, trousers and ponchos.

African textiles and clothes were especially popular with black Americans, whose interest in African cultures grew alongside the Civil Rights movement. The first celebration of Kwanzaa in 1966 heralded an era of black American culture that was no longer a derivative of white America, but rather a celebration of African heritage. In September 1966, *Life* magazine featured New York designer Khadejha (her birth name was Erva Holmes), who used African printed cloth to make summer shifts and patio-style jumpsuits with cut-out midriffs. Khadejha had begun her business in 1963 designing fashion for women in her own community, but by 1966 she was selling to over fifty

stores across the country, and not just among the black population. By 1968, 'Afro' fashions were being worn for daily attire in America, especially the dashiki. In Harlem, The New Breed was one of many boutiques that specialized in Afro-style clothing in the belief that black style could become commercially viable in a broader marketplace. The look extended to jewelry and especially hairstyles; Diahann Carroll and Diana Ross both sported Afros in 1968, although in wig form.

In Britain, a new wave of fashion designers were on the rise: Ossie Clark, Zandra Rhodes and Thea Porter created 'ethnostalgic' fashions that fused nostalgic and ethnographic prints, patterns and palettes. The styles of boutiques were changing and failure was possible if the owner didn't keep pace with the market or treat their business seriously. This was never more apparent than in the brief history of the Beatles' own venture into fashion with their Apple Boutique.

In September 1967 the Beatles decided to open a fashion boutique as the first venture of their newly founded Apple Corps empire. The boutique would be located at 94 Baker Street in London, a property the band's accountants had already acquired

as a long-term investment. Pattie Boyd suggested they hire a design collective called The Fool to create the clothes. Boyd had already modelled some pieces created by Josje Leeger, one of the partners in The Fool. The other partners included Marijke Koeger and her husband Simon Posthuma. They had originally owned a boutique called The Trend in Amsterdam that had been successful until financial mismanagement caused it to close. The group eventually settled in London where they teamed up with another designer, Barry Finch.

The Beatles gave The Fool £100,000 to stock the new Apple Boutique and decorate the exterior of the shop. Things started off badly when the building was painted in a three-storey psychedelic mural that immediately generated complaints from neighbouring merchants. The following spring Westminster Council required the building to be painted over, which it was – in pure white. The interior layout of the store was being organized by the Beatles themselves, but as shop manager Pete Shotton soon discovered, he had four bosses all with different ideas but for one thing: that everything in the shop had to be for sale, including fixtures and fittings!

Workrooms had been established above the shop, where the psychedelic medieval-inspired clothes could be made using thousands of pounds' worth of silk and velvet fabric. Once made, every piece would then have a multicoloured woven silk label whose production cost was higher than the retail price of some of the clothes. Shotton brought this issue to John Lennon's attention but was told, 'Oh, let them do what they want. We're not business freaks, we're artists...if we don't make any money, what does it matter?'

The shop opened in the first week of December 1967 with a staff that included a gypsy, a narcoleptic self-proclaimed mystic

Above: English astronomical-themed boots by CHELSEA COBBLER, 1968.

Right: American floral-embroidered boots by JERRY EDOUARD, *c.* 1970.

Opposite left: English hippies on their way to Woburn Abbey music festival, August 1967.

Opposite right: Illustrations from 'A Hip Fashion Guide', from *The Hippie's Handbook: How to Live on Love*, by Ruth Bronsteen, published in September 1967, when the Summer of Love was winding down. The author says hippies are 'sympathetic, bright, aware, unpretentious, naive, direct, open and unrealistic'. But she also notes that they are 'clannish and provincial in their hippiedom', 'concerned with postures and appearances', as well as 'completely self-absorbed'.

Right: American wet-look vinyl trousers and vest outfit, *c.* 1969–70. The peace sign was created as a symbol for nuclear disarmament in 1958, but by the mid-1960s it had become an icon of the hippie generation.

Below left: American purple-and-red suede-fringed vest and PETER MAX print jeans, *c.* 1970. Native American Indian clothing inspired the fringed leather vest and headband – icons of hippie style.

Below right: Beach cover-up of printed terry cloth featuring hippie slang: 'Turn On', 'Peace', 'Love' and 'Flipped Out', *c.* 1968–69.

Above: Hippie-influenced
mainstream fashion: Indian
embroidered suede dress, 1969.

Right: Paisley-print cotton dress,
Canada, *c.* 1967–69.

and a handful of inexperienced shop girls who didn't know how to deal with problems like shoplifters. The stock was a little behind the times and many trinkets were already stocked by other London boutiques. Shotton quit. The new manager immediately recognized that one of the problems was The Fool, who were taking stock and charging debts to Apple. The Beatles decided it would cause too much embarrassment to take legal action and dropped the matter.

Despite all these issues, the company expanded in February 1968 when John Crittle, owner of the shop Dandy Fashions, went into business with the Beatles. Crittle's store was renamed Apple Tailoring in May 1968, but just two months later the Beatles ended the partnership when they realized their boutique experiment had been a financial disaster that had cost them nearly £200,000.

Rather than liquidate the stock through regular means, they gave everything away for free – the stock, the fabric, the fixtures and fittings – anything, that is, that Lennon and Yoko Ono hadn't been able to fit into the back of their Rolls-Royce the night before. There were no limits to what could be taken, until one woman began prying up the carpet.

The year 1968 was unrelentingly packed with news of wars, protests, raids, riots and assassinations around the world. In response to a demonstration in Central Park in New York during which an American flag was burned in protest of the war in Vietnam, US Congress passed the Federal Flag Desecration Law, which banned any display of contempt towards the flag. Soon there were news stories of over-zealous officials enforcing the new law. Police requested an upscale boutique in Bridgehampton, New York, to cease selling a French-made shirt printed with a Stars and Stripes motif because it 'desecrated the American flag'. Deanna Littell dropped her plans to design a flag-inspired jacket for Paraphernalia after she learned the Daughters of the American Revolution had brought a suit against a manufacturer for producing a patriotically patterned girdle.

The politically oriented 'yippies', founded at the end of 1967 and named after the acronym for Youth International Party, were known for their media attention-grabbing antics. Yippies often conspicuously used clothing, or lack thereof, as a form of protest. Leaders Abbie Hoffman and Jerry Rubin were particularly known for using their dress to make political statements, especially while being tried as part of the Chicago Eight – a group of protestors who were blamed for inciting a riot at the Democratic National Convention in August 1968.

In October 1968, while trying to interrupt a meeting on un-American activities in Washington DC, Abbie Hoffman was arrested for wearing a shirt that resembled the American flag. When Hoffman's case came to court, his defence attorney asked the court, 'Is wearing a shirt dishonoring the flag? Does Uncle Sam, when he marches in the parade on July 4th, dishonor?' After the judge declared him guilty, Hoffman said, in words borrowed from Revolutionary War hero Nathan Hale, 'I only regret that I have but one shirt to give for my country.'

Interpretation of the flag law, desecration versus patriotism, and free speech became hotly debated topics. The controversy actually fuelled a fashion for Stars and Stripes patterns among those who questioned the legality of the law under the First Amendment for free speech. A final ruling came down in 1972 after a youth was arrested in Massachusetts for wearing a flag patch on the seat of his trousers. The Supreme Court ruled in favour of the youth due to ambiguity in the definition of contempt within the Flag Desecration Law and its conflict with the First Amendment. The ruling left plenty of time for American flag-inspired clothing to saturate the market for Bicentennial celebrations in 1976.

Boutiques were everywhere during 1968 and 1969. Helene Robertson, owner since 1962 of Anastasia's boutique in Sausalito, California, had followed the trends from mod to hippie, and lamented in an article for *Rags* in February 1971, 'A boutique used to be where you could find something out of the ordinary, something that had a little attention given to it…. It's not that way any more. There are too many boutiques. There's a glut on the market…. Even the department stores have gotten hip and have special boutique sections.' In New York, Bergdorf Goodman had opened Bigi – a teen-oriented boutique that was expanded in early 1969 in both size and scope – aimed at college-aged women as well as teens. Similarly, Bonwit Teller had the S'fari Room, aimed at the boutique-buying younger market.

In 1968 the leading boutiques in Los Angeles were Bootstrings, Rose Revived, Skitzo-My Generation, The Game of Works, Chequer West, The Candy Happening and Sat Purush; and in New York Abracadabra, Okefenokee, Opening Line, The Stitching Horse, Hindu Khush, Intergalactic Trading Post, Once Upon a Time, Grizzly Furs, Sunita's Boutique Plastique, Splendiferous, The What Not Shop, Limbo, Serendipity, Dakota Transit and Paraphernalia. Competition for business was stiff as more stores opened, and cheaper line-for-line knock-offs that appeared in department stores hurt small boutiques. Mod had become too diffuse and mainstream to be considered cool

enough for a boutique. Paraphernalia, which had launched in New York in late 1965 to great success, had, by the end of 1968, expanded to forty-four locations across the US, mostly as shops within department stores, but sales were flattening as the business wasn't staying on top of changing tastes and times. The partners, Paul Young and Carl Rosen, had a falling out; the chain went public, Rosen pulled out and the Paraphernalia franchises slowly closed over the next decade. Betsey Johnson, who had parted ways with Paraphernalia in 1968, started a boutique with two partners in early 1969 called Betsey Bunky & Nini, but when she realized there was no real future for small boutiques she sought out a more secure arrangement with a junior sportswear firm, for which she began designing a line in early 1970 under the Alley Cat label.

Marcia Flanders of the Abracadabra boutique in New York commented in a February 1971 interview for *Rags*, 'Things have changed, you know. People have a kind of social consciousness now. They don't give a shit about clothes – they're

Far left: American flag-inspired flared-leg trousers, originally purchased and worn in the San Francisco/Berkeley area in 1968 and 1969.

Left: Leading yippie Abbie Hoffman being arrested in October 1968 for wearing a US flag-inspired shirt.

really frivolous and unimportant. There was a time when Abracadabra was first open, when everybody was going to discotheques, and they wanted to be seen in some way-out outfit every night. But nobody's anyplace any more. They're staying home and getting into themselves…. I'm just not getting off on clothes any more. Dressing silly people in silly clothes doesn't seem very important.'

In 1970 *Rags* reported that Janis Joplin had voiced a similar sentiment in 1968: 'Like, man, I really don't give a damn about clothes…. Basically clothes are a façade, nothing more. I groove on my clothes now because I have to. I'm entertaining in front of an audience and I have to care how I look, regardless of how I really feel…. The secret is freedom and that means no bras or girdles. You got to do what you want to do and wear what you want to wear…. But the big question is, is it matching your soul?'

Despite her lack of interest in fashion, as a celebrity, her style was influential. 'She created the Hip-Earth Mother/ Sex Symbol image,' said Blair Sabol, writer for *Rags*, in December 1970. 'She became a hairstyle: "Give me a Janis Joplin."'

A certain tie-dye velvet was named after her and advertised as "The Joplin Lightning Motif". It is said that she increased the sale of the "mule" style of slipper by 100 per cent in 1968…. Janis made funk a fashion.' Similarly, Jimi Hendrix was a fashion icon, as much as one existed for the hippie movement. In 1968 Hendrix began tying scarves to one leg and one arm, and by mid-1969 was wearing bandana headbands and fringed leather clothing – styles that were avidly copied by both sexes, especially after his appearance at the biggest American music festival of the hippie age, Woodstock.

Bolstered by political causes and unified by music, from folk to psychedelic rock, the movement maintained its focus into the early 1970s through protests and music festivals. The hippie generation entered the decade strongly but began dissipating after the deaths of Jimi Hendrix and Janis Joplin in the autumn of 1970. The music festivals dwindled in attendance, and by the time the US pulled out of Vietnam in early 1973, the hippie generation had all but disappeared into a sea of blue jeans and T-shirts – the uniform of early 1970s youth.

Above: Dutch patchwork coat made from worn and faded American jeans with rhinestone and metal stud decoration spelling out 'For Denim Life Time', purchased from a street vendor in Amsterdam, *c.* 1970–71.

Left: American cotton twill trouser suit with photo print of the crowd at Woodstock, *c.* 1970–71.

LIFE

FULBRIGHT: ENIGMA OF THE MAN

LYNDA BIRD'S HOLLYWOOD FLAME

FACE IT! Revolution in Male Clothes

Chicago school students
take to new mod gear

MAY 13 · 1966 · 40¢

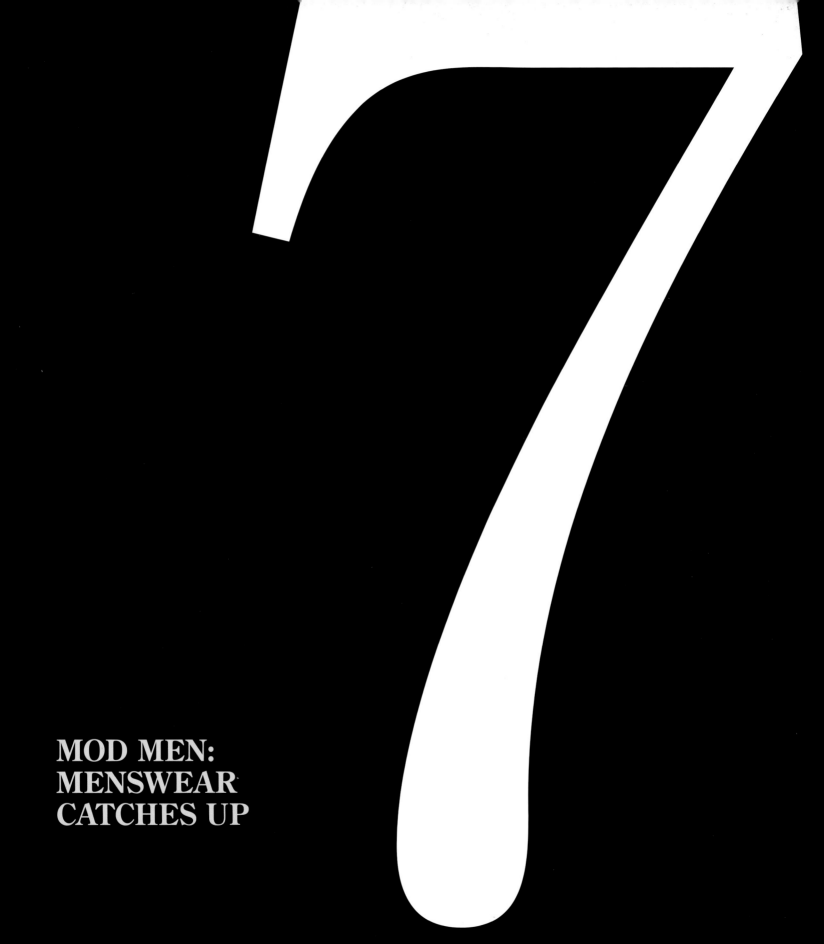

MOD MEN:
MENSWEAR
CATCHES UP

'What we would like to see is men dressing more to the limits of their own personality and inventiveness…'

Gentlemen's Quarterly, February 1965

Life ran a snippet in May 1960 about how the pocket handkerchief could be folded into a peak for a more modern look, rather than the old-fashioned four points. This suggestion is indicative of the tiny modifications that had occurred in the man's wardrobe since the 1910s. Business and evening suits were almost entirely insulated from influential trends and only slowly changed in appearance through subtle alterations in the narrowing and widening of lapels, ties and trouser legs. The most important function of men's clothes was to create an appearance of masculinity and respectability. For a young executive who wanted to advance his career, a flamboyant tie might give the impression of effeminacy, or a beard could end his prospects if his superiors thought he looked like a beatnik or a Bolshevik.

Even casual styles were slow to change. A Fred Perry or Lacoste polo shirt was a weekend wardrobe basic that exhibited no major alteration in style for decades. Likewise, a zip-front Baracuta windbreaker or a pair of plaid Bermuda shorts looked much the same season after season. Unlike women's fashions, men's clothes did not fall out of style easily and were only updated as needed due to size or wear.

In the February 1965 issue of American magazine *Gentlemen's Quarterly*, a full-page photo featured a man in a business suit with a large 'X' drawn over him. The editor declared: 'His dark suit fits well and is neatly pressed. The white of his shirt collar and cuffs makes their proper appearance at the neck and sleeves, and his trousers just touch his shoes. His tie does not clash…. The outfit is not dated or rumpled or poorly coordinated. It just happens to be dull. To believe that all there is to dressing is to be neat and clean is stultifying to a man with any creative urge…. What we would like to see is men dressing more to the limits of their own personality and inventiveness instead of following the patterns of dress set by other men in their professional or social milieu….'

The revolution had begun.

CREAZIONI SPECIALI
REDMAN
FRATELLI CERRUTI 1881

TEDD

... la préférence
marquée par quelques-uns
des meilleurs tailleurs

Left: The Italian-French firm of CERRUTI was one of the first to infuse a touch of youthful styling into conservative suit styles with a narrowed waist, higher arm hole and broader shoulder, spring 1965.

In the US, the young President Kennedy was influencing American men's business fashion in 1961 with the 'JFK Look', a two-button single-breasted suit worn without a hat. The 'Britisher' style of suit jacket with a higher three-button closure was the only other alternative for young men. The avant-garde could choose a suit by Pierre Cardin, who showed his first men's collection in 1960 and offered a conspicuously modern-styled collarless jacket that he called the Cylinder. Cardin's suit utilized traditional tailoring stripped of all details and tapered to 'suit' the younger male physique. Nobody wore it, but the style opened the door to the influence of trend over tradition in menswear.

Around the same time, London's mods were reviving the idea of the dandy. The mods were interested in fashion and spent what money they had on their appearance. Bespoke was still the usual way most men bought their better clothes in the UK, but a taste for the exotic led many mods to seek out Italian sharkskin suits (sharkskin was a two-tone mohair wool with a sheen that showed different colours from different angles). Fashion was vital; being out of step with style was a mod disgrace. Those who weren't right up to date with the latest look were called Tickets or States, as in 'He's a first-class ticket,' or 'She's in a bit of a state.'

Just two blocks away from London's Savile Row, where some of the finest suits were custom made for the British establishment, was Carnaby Street – soon to become the meridian of mod. Carnaby was just a narrow run-down lane behind the London Palladium before John Stephen (aka the 'King of Carnaby Street') and his partner Bill Franks opened His Clothes at No. 5 in 1957. The shop became known for its bright yellow exterior, loud music and affordable, stylish merchandise, such as suits with short double-breasted jackets called 'bum-freezers' (ideal for wearing while driving a scooter), and hipster

Far left: Conservative and masculine styling: model from fashion show, Yorkdale mall, Toronto, 1965.

Left: Interior of the Mr Fish boutique, Clifford Street, London, c. 1968.

Opposite left: Collarless jackets and slim trousers, Simpsons-Sears, Canada, autumn/winter 1965.

Opposite right: The Beatle boot and its variations, Eaton's catalogue, Canada, spring/summer 1966.

trousers, although many modsters found that style a bit too effete – at first.

In the September 1962 edition of *Town* magazine, an interview appeared with fifteen-year-old Mark Feld (later known as Marc Bolan of T-Rex fame). As an 'Ace Face', Mark Feld and his associates bought from His Clothes, as well as from clothiers John Michael and Harry Fenton. 'You got to be two steps ahead…. The stuff that half the haddocks you see around wearing I was wearing years ago. A kid in my class came up to me in his new suit, an Italian box it was…I was wearing that style two years ago,' said Feld.

That December the Beatles were being toffed up for publicity shots in the wake of the moderate success of their first song release in the UK. Dougie Millings, an established Compton Street tailor who had already created looks for other rising music stars, was hired to polish the rocker look off the Liverpool four. Millings created a Modernist style with his version of the collarless Cylinder jacket made up in the mods' preferred fabric, Italian mohair, instead of the more egalitarian corduroy that Cardin had used.

With mod culture gaining momentum, John Stephen's Carnaby Street business expanded to fifteen stores in just a few years. By 1964 Stephen was offering everything from Ben Sherman shirts to a 'John Stephen' brand of ready-made clothes from a Glasgow manufacturer. Stephen realized that, although he might be competing against himself, a sale would eventually occur in one of his boutiques, and it all went into the same cashbox. In a December 1967 interview in *Town* magazine he said, 'Carnaby is my creation…. I feel about it the same way Michelangelo felt about the beautiful statues he created.'

An article in a Vancouver newspaper from February 1964 outlined young men's fashion from the point of view of someone

Ten great EATON BRAEMORE styles that give you more dollar value

unfamiliar with the mod scene: 'In the Kingdom of Mod the young men are the peacocks of the land…. The boys wear long, slightly fitted jackets, Cuban heel…boots and straight from the knee slim pants…. And this should take what's left of your breath away, some of the Mod boys are experimenting with a bit of eye make-up.'

The look crossed the Atlantic with the British music invasion. But while young women took to English mod style, young men didn't jump as quickly, preferring the endemic American look of jeans and sweatshirts worn with tennis shoes. The newest American innovation for young men's casual clothing were Jams, a cropped pyjama pant (the forerunner of board shorts) invented by surfing enthusiast Dave Rochlen, that swept across the US from Hawaii to California and eastwards in 1965.

By 1966 the mod look was finally catching on. *Life* reported on the revolution in men's fashion coming to the US from Britain in its 13 May 1966 issue: 'The man who led the young clothes revolution in England and is fomenting it now in the US is 29-year-old John Stephen…he made a success with tight, hip-slung trousers, based on the American blue jean. Worn with a turtleneck sweater, this became the uniform of the Mod, the fashion-mad, newly affluent English youth…. His clothes have already done well in the US and by fall will be sold in 17 American department stores. France's rival to Stephen…is the renowned couturier Pierre Cardin…Bonwit Teller plans to introduce Cardin's clothes to the US this fall.'

Just as mod was becoming influential in the US in 1966 it was becoming more extreme in London, where the latest look was the aesthetic dandy: velvet-collared double-breasted frock coats, polka-dot patterned shirts, wide floral ties with over-sized knots, lace cravats and ruffled cuffs. This style from the past was coming from new men's boutiques like Mr Fish, which opened in 1966 on Clifford Street, near Carnaby. Early in 1966, The Kinks released the song 'A Dedicated Follower

Right: Green wool suit labelled 'STRICKLAND AND SONS LTD., 15 Savile Row, London' and dated 17 March 1970.

Far right: Wool topcoat labelled 'SPORTIVE – MALE BY PAUL – 39 and 47 Carnaby Street, London.' Made for export, c. 1966–68.

Below: Brocade silk-and-wool evening tuxedo labelled 'JOE FELLER, Ottawa, Canada' and dated 10 June 1969.

of Fashion', which poked fun at the 'Carnebetian army' of mod peacocks who followed every fickle fad featured in London's boutiques, from polka dots one week to stripes the next.

American clothing manufacturers were adding mod style to their autumn 1966 men's collections. Bestsellers included low-rise hip-hugging slacks and wide-wale corduroys with bell bottoms; floral-print shirts with high white collars and cuffs; 'Dutch boy' or trainman caps in cloth or leather (later called the Nureyev cap in honour of the famous ballet star who defected to the West); extra-wide paisley and polka-dot ties; turtleneck sweaters; and double-breasted sport coats with deep side vents. Turtlenecks worn under jackets were becoming especially popular with the young, although many restaurants refused to seat men without a tie.

The more daring could wear a jewel-tone velvet suit with a Nehru jacket. Inspired by the Chinese 'Mao collar' jacket, the standing collar style was originated in 1965 by the Paris *tailleur*

Gilbert Feruch. American fashion sources shifted the style away from the Communist Chinese reference to Jawaharlal Nehru, the first prime minister of India, who had worn the sherwani, a similar-looking traditional closed-neck coat. Despite general praise from the fashion world for the Nehru jacket it had fallen from popularity by 1969, partly because it was not dissimilar in style to uniform jackets worn by train stewards, hotel bellhops or members of a marching band.

Other eccentric fashion ideas that came and went quickly included caftans, capes, walking sticks and, for the greatest shock value – miniskirts. *Life* reported on 11 August 1967 that 'miniskirts for men have begun showing up in Paris, Munich, London and Tokyo. In Scotland the minikilt raised the line to nine inches above the knee. In Japan the outfits include tops and can be worn by both men and women.' Miniskirts for men were just another of those headline-seeking fads and never seriously considered as a real fashion; however, they did open up the possibility of unisex styling – as long as it was women who adapted menswear and not the other way around.

Unisex styles were being touted as the 'in' thing in early 1968. Trouser suits with various jacket styles were especially popular choices, as were vests and printed jeans. Beauty products also went unisex, but advertising kept male grooming manly to remove any hint of 'sissiness': skin bronzers, toners and creams were sold as 'before' and 'after' shaving products, and colognes and deodorants were aimed to appeal to the 'women in your life'. Men were also growing facial hair, especially sideburns, and were having their hair styled and dyed at men's salons, rather than cut and shaved by barbers. *Life* magazine first reported on the trend for men's hair styling salons over barbershops in their 30 July 1965 edition, noting that men were growing their hair longer because of the Beatles, and quoting a college oarsmen as saying, 'Not even members of crews have crew cuts.'

A turn towards the nostalgic had started with a nod to 1930s gangsters after the success of the film *Bonnie and Clyde* in autumn 1967. Men's business suits became shapelier with broader shoulders, narrower waists and flared jacket skirts and trouser legs. Off-the-rack 'designer' suits were a new reality with bestselling styles by Pierre Cardin, Oleg Cassini, Hardy Amies, Valentino and Bill Blass. Stodgy businessmen began wearing subtly patterned and coloured shirts with four-inch-wide ties, and fewer men were wearing hats, but those who did wore broader brims, and to provide balance in the outfit shoes also began to grow wider.

The vintage trend had strengthened by 1969 with a sharper silhouette recreated through squared shoulders, broad lapels, wide trousers with turn-up cuffs and Art Deco-print ties. Bill Blass advocated dark shirts and ties worn with a suit in a loud plaid, and jackets cut higher in the armhole to make the man over forty 'look thinner and stay thinner'. Another vintage look for 1969 was the safari jacket from Yves Saint Laurent, often worn with a neck scarf.

Less successful styles for 1969 included men's fur coats that only a handful of male celebrities bought, including American football star Joe Namath. Odder fashions included sheer-fabric shirts and the shoulder-strapped manbag. Both styles were considered effete, especially in light of the gay movement that burst out of the closet during the summer of 1969. Surprisingly, sheer shirts had healthy sales; but, although the manbag found some success in Europe, there were few takers in North America.

Just when it seemed that dandyism was on the decline, there was a revival in 1970 that included fringed leather vests and coats, printed jeans, long scarves and jewelry. *Life* pointed out in September 1970 that 'most designers credit the distinctly undandy hippies with making possible the return to dandyism, simply by proving that a fellow can wear almost any outlandish costume in public – if he has the nerve....'

BEAUTY FROM THE NECK UP: HAIR AND COSMETICS

8

'"Girls" don't wear hats, but women – the well-dressed ones – do for all outdoor occasions…. No outfit is complete without a hat!'

Abigail van Buren, 'Dear Abby' column, November 1963

For his spring 1958 fashion show, Paris couturier Givenchy had his models' hair styled close to their heads so they could wear hats with his daytime clothes; when they reappeared in evening wear later in the show, they were hatless with their hair back-combed into fluffy bouffant styles to complement Givenchy's bubble-shaped skirts. Due to the lack of time available to restyle their hair between day and evening outfits, the transformation was achieved by the use of wigs. Givenchy's collection was a hit that spring and women were soon dressing their hair in bouffant styles, often by wearing wigs. However, real-hair wigs cost between $250 and $400 (the equivalent of about $2,000 to $3,000 today), with blonde being the most expensive. The only way to justify the purchase of a wig would be to amortize the cost in time and money spent at the hairdresser. In 1962 Dynel synthetic wigs hit the market at an affordable $50, and they took off in popularity that summer, especially with women who had problems retaining the bounce and curl of their own hair in humidity.

For women who wanted the bouffant style but not in a wig, hairspray was necessary to freeze the tossed and teased locks into place. It had been on the market only a few years when the bouffant came into fashion, but as hairstyles grew larger so did hairspray sales; *Life* magazine reported that revenues in 1960 topped $81 million in the US. Accompanying the big hairspray sales and the big hairstyles were big-name hairdressers: Alexandre de Paris, Kenneth of New York and René of London were the mane celebrities.

Although popular, the bouffant was not universal. Norman Norell's autumn 1960 collection in New York was inspired by the 1920s, complete with models wearing short, shingled hair complemented by pale face powder and charcoal-blackened eyelids. Adding further to the 1920s look, a spit curl curved over the cheek became popular that winter. The 1961 French nouvelle vague film *Last Year at Marienbad* (released in the US in spring 1962) was even more influential in promoting

Manteau de
PIERRE CARDIN
en lainage réversible
de
CHATILLON-MOULY-ROUSSEL

1920s hairstyles when the heroine, played by Delphine Seyrig, appeared in a sleek, short, close-fitted coiffure with bangs swept to one side. The style was admired for being refreshingly young with artless sophistication. Popularized in the US by New York socialite Gloria Vanderbilt, the Marienbad cut led the way for shorter hairstyles.

For those preferring big hair, the ancient vamp look of Cleopatra arrived in the summer of 1962. Dark, heavy bangs with a sculpted and lacquered bouffant that mimicked ancient Egyptian wigs were worn with thick eyeliner extending towards the temples. The fashion anticipated the release of the epic film about the ancient queen starring Elizabeth Taylor, but by the time the movie debuted the following year, the fad was long gone.

Many women were going hatless for most occasions in the early 1960s, but the problem of hats crushing inflated bouffant hairdos put milliners and hairdressers at odds. Women with shorter hair, or who pinned up their longer hair, could wear a variety of slouch-brimmed hats, turbans of swirled tulle or satin, and cloche styles exploding in ice-cream-hued flowers for spring or made up in strong coloured felts for winter to capture the 1920s look. The newest addition in millinery was Pierre Cardin's 'Sou'wester' hat – a Paris hit for spring 1961 that consisted of a deep-crowned cloche with downturned brim swooping to the shoulders at the back.

The bouffant bubble burst in 1963, allowing milliners to get back to business, and the battle of milliners versus hairdressers was in full swing during 1963 and 1964. While hairdressers were busy convincing women that cocktail hats were passé and that hair should be swept up high with a postiche to become a feature of the evening ensemble, tempting daytime hats flooded the market. Paris preferred interesting shapes like

Right: Straw pillbox by BALENCIAGA, Paris, c. 1960.

Below: Velvet square-brim hat by MR. JOHN, New York, c. 1964–65.

Opposite, clockwise from top left: PAULETTE's version of HALSTON'S scarf hat, Paris, 1967; riding helmet-inspired hat by JEAN PATOU, Paris, 1964; ocelot cap by JEAN BERTHET, Paris, 1964; floral turban by GILBERT ORCEL, Paris, 1966.

a reinterpretation of the pith helmet in white felt, or mini-bowlers, called *melon* in French.

The millinery industry had been fighting to survive for years, reportedly pleading with First Lady Jacqueline Kennedy to wear more hats to encourage American women to do the same. Hat-wearing fan Constance Woodworth of the *New York Journal-American* wrote a column on 21 April 1963 entitled 'Missing Millinery' in which she tattled on a number of well-known New York fashion personalities who had attended luncheons at smart restaurants hatless; names included *Harper's Bazaar* fabric and fur editor Eve Orton and *Vogue* editor Cathy di Montezemolo.

'A woman can go anywhere hatless, with the exception of certain churches,' said Amy Vanderbilt in her 1963 revised *Complete Book of Etiquette*. Abigail Van Buren's 'Dear Abby' column was less forgiving in a response to a writer asking whether she should wear a hat to a football game in November 1963: '"Girls" don't wear hats, but women – the well-dressed ones – do for all outdoor occasions from garden parties to football games…. No outfit is complete without a hat!' But even the milliner Frederic Hirst of the John-Frederics salon admitted in the May 1963 issue of *Hats*: 'Hats have become a complete accessory…unless the hat…is functional like beach or rainwear….'

Milliners were hopeful in spring 1964 when Hats reported in its April issue, 'Paris, Rome and London are behaving as though hats are the greatest thing since the cotton gin.' Sears in the US offered mail-order hats from America's biggest names in millinery: Emme, Sally Victor, Mr. John and Lilly Daché. *Life* reported on the collection in its 20 March issue: 'Their designs are in keeping with the stark anti-flower trim in Paris. More conspicuous than the little perched pillbox, these hats are worn straight on the crown and often frame the face with curving brims. They also go with fashionable straight hair…. These designs may stem the tide of hatlessness which has engulfed milliners….'

The trend for headwear continued into autumn 1964. All the European couture collections featured hats; in New York, Norell showed sixty with his autumn collection. Both Bill Blass and Geoffrey Beene proclaimed their love of hats in an August 1964 Hats article, noting that the young were even beginning to wear them. Milliners loved the news from Paris, where designer Jacques Esterel proclaimed that 'women are imprisoned by their own hair'; to combat this incarceration he planned to shave the hair off several of his models, perching hats on top of their hairless heads for his autumn couture collection. Esterel apparently never followed through – his bravado was just another publicity stunt following the 'topless' rage of 1964 that had begun with the monokini.

Halston of Bergdorf Goodman created the hat to have for spring 1965, consisting of a scarf wrapped over a conically shaped net dome for a medieval peasant look. However, other than Halston's hit, hat wearing was on the slide again. Formal hats had not caught on with the young, who equated fussy styles with being 'square' and 'middle aged'. Younger women would wear squashy caps with visor brims, and berets, but the era of dressy hats and gloves was over. In the December 1967 issue of *Hats*, the doyenne of American millinery, Lilly Daché, said the age of hats had passed and that hair was more important. She refused to mourn the passing of her industry and admitted she seldom wore a hat any more: 'I'm not going to make myself conspicuous,' she said.

What young women wanted instead of hats were smart haircuts, and short shingled bobs had been increasing in popularity since the film *Last Year at Marienbad* came out in 1962. By the end of 1963, English hair cutter Vidal Sassoon was becoming known at his London salon for creating short geometric-shaped haircuts that mod designer Mary Quant sported. By the summer of 1965 when Sassoon opened a branch in New York, his five-point haircut with heavy bangs sitting low on the eyebrows and very little else behind was a vital ingredient for mod chic.

'Bebe' bonnet, a style of close-fitting hood with chin strap, introduced by COURRÈGES in 1965, rendered in tartan with an optional Breton brim, by New York milliner EMME, *c.* 1965–67.

Above: Leather rounded pillbox with chin strap by ADOLFO, New York, c. 1965–66.

Left: Quilted leather helmet with clear plastic visor by GIGI OF FLORENCE, c. 1966–67.

Right and below: Hiroko Matsumoto modelling PIERRE CARDIN garments and hats, including a wide-brimmed Breton from spring 1966, and a hood from autumn 1966. PIERRE CARDIN discovered Hiroko Matsumoto in Japan and brought her to Paris to model his clothes in 1960.

The Sassoon cut was not for the faint of heart, and for those who rued the loss of their locks, the 'fall' arrived in late spring 1966. The fall was a hairpiece of straight hair worn loose down the back, often with the heavy bangs of a Sassoon cut. Falls suited a wide age range of women, and for evening several could be braided together to create enormous, glamorous hairstyles interwoven with ribbons and flowers. Worn short or long, hairstyles were designed for girlish appeal and, in keeping with that aesthetic, the figure was becoming more sylph-like: Jean Shrimpton, Twiggy and Penelope Tree were the preference of high-fashion photographers. Their girlish chic was enhanced by make-up that made their eyes as large as possible. The big-eyed look was generally credited to French beauty Brigitte Bardot at the beginning of the decade, who reportedly began wearing beat-inspired heavy eyeliner to distract attention from her thick lips. The effect on Bardot was very sensual, and emphasizing the eyes over other facial features created a youthful appearance that was eagerly copied. With heavier eyeliner, wider swathes of coloured shadow and false eyelashes soon followed.

Pablo Manzoni, known as just 'Pablo', was the star of high-fashion eye make-up. He had started at Elizabeth Arden's Rome salon before being brought to New York, where he won a Coty American Fashion Critics' Award in autumn 1965 for elevating the art of make-up through his inventive use of coloured false eyelashes, eyeliner, shadow, and whatever else appealed to him – from feathers to rhinestones.

As eyes were getting bigger with make-up, sunglasses also grew in popularity. Sales more than doubled in the first five years of the 1960s according to an article in the 4 June 1965 issue of *Life*: '...the more that the eyes appear big-big-googly, the more "in" the glasses are.' By early 1966, granny chic was on the rise and old-fashioned wire frames were becoming popular – *Life* pointed out in a 4 February article, 'It really doesn't matter whether you need to wear glasses. It doesn't even matter whether the frames have lenses in them. What matters is that the glasses look downright owlish. They can be authentic antiques searched out in junk shops and enterprising boutiques or they can be modern copies....' Wire-frame glasses were popular with hippies too.

The artificiality of high-fashion hairdos in the beginning and middle of the 1960s inspired a rebirth of naturalism at the end of the decade. Influenced by the hippie movement, more women, and men, were letting their hair grow long, and naturally straight or curly. However, despite the rejection of artificiality, wigs grew in popularity in the late 1960s and early 1970s, taking the place of hats in the wardrobe.

Left: Wig and box by JEROME ALEXANDER, *c.* 1969. Balding was not the only reason for men to take up wigs. Reservists with shaven heads wore wigs to blend in with civilians, as did men with long locks who worked in conservative environments.

Opposite: Mary Quant and Vidal Sassoon, 1965.

AFTERSHOCK:
FASHION IN THE
LATE 1960s

'Nowadays the doorman doesn't know who to let in.'

Marshall McLuhan, *Rags*, October 1970

For his spring/summer 1968 couture collection, Valentino Garavani, known simply as Valentino, created romantic, feminine dresses in shades of white. Valentino's loyal following included Mrs Robert Kennedy, who first came to him in 1962 when she required a black gown on short notice for a papal audience. Jacqueline Kennedy was also a fan of Valentino's clothes, and if his name was not yet well known, that would change after she wore one of his spring 1968 white dresses for her marriage to Aristotle Onassis that October. Her dress had a ladylike above-the-knee pleated skirt, high-necked blouse with full sleeves and deep cuffs, and bands of lace undulating across the bodice and sleeves.

Valentino set up shop in Rome in 1960 and produced couture long after most other designers had shifted their industry to high-end ready-to-wear. By the late 1960s Milan, rather than Florence or Rome, had become the seat of Italian fashion – the city where manufacturing, not art or history, was the leading industry. It was in luxury ready-to-wear that Italian companies like Krizia, Missoni, Gucci and Roberta di Camerino excelled and became leading brands in the 1970s.

Nostalgic romanticism and space-age futurism coexisted as fashion influences in the late 1960s, but after the American space program put men on the moon in July 1969, the interest in futurism waned. Of the leading Modernists, Courrèges and Cardin adapted their visions while Gernreich, who believed in a future where everyone would wear unisex leotards or kaftans and purchase clothes via the television, scoffed that 'America is afraid of the future, so we're going back to the past – wearing costumes', as reported in a 1981 *People* magazine retrospective. Gernreich closed up his business at the end of 1968 and went into semi-retirement, continuing his contract with Harmon knits into the 1970s.

Every designer in the world had followed the hemline's upward trajectory by spring 1968. Mary Quant proclaimed the

Right: COURRÈGES-style crisp
tailoring for the futuristic look
by JEAN-MARIE ARMAND, Paris,
Autumn 1968.

Opposite left: Sculpted wool shifts by PIERRE CARDIN, Paris, spring 1968.

Opposite right: Green wool and PVC vinyl dress by PIERRE CARDIN,

Opposite, top left: A return to romance and ruffles for spring: window display at Franklin Simon, New York, April 1968.

Opposite, bottom left: Romantic Italian lace outfit by ANTONELLI, Rome, autumn 1968.

Opposite right: American ruffled silk chiffon dress, unlabelled, spring 1968.

Right: Tailored wool coat with full skirt, VALENTINO, Rome, autumn 1968.

miniskirt 'a fashion classic that will never be replaced' in a *St Petersburg Times* article on 26 March. But alternatives were already becoming popular. The 'costumes' Gernreich was referring to were old-fashioned looks with longer hemlines and demure styling. Lace, velvet and chiffon were on the increase; ruffled blouses with high collars looked their nostalgic best when worn with calf-length midi skirts, although few women were smitten by midis at first.

The 1930s styling of the film *Bonnie and Clyde* had been a strong influence behind the return of sweater coats, midi skirts, gangster-style striped suiting, lace-up shoes, and chiffon dinner dresses with bows and scarves at the throat in the autumn 1967 collections. *Life* reported in its 12 January 1968 issue, 'Actress Faye Dunaway…has already done for the beret what Bardot did for the bikini. Now the fashion world's newest darling is the stunning inspiration for a full-blast return to 30s styles, both here and abroad. Though revivals have cropped up before, it took the impact of the film to bring about a new synthesis that blends the softness and droopy fit of the 30s with the swing and legginess of the 60s.'

In France, young women were reportedly storming the boutiques for longer skirts after the film was released there in late January 1968. *Life* reported on 16 February, 'What's up – or down – with skirt lengths these days? Norman Norell stirred up a commotion last month by dropping some hemlines to mid-calf, but he also showed an undogmatic spectrum of

hemlines…. The attitude of the fashion world is one of gentle permissiveness, and all the arbiters are agreed that the new lengths are in addition to, not instead of, the mini. They are all also agreed that the downward trend improves the status of a nameless length that hovers at the knee and which during the rise of the mini was dismissed as drearily dowdy. In general, the feeling is for peaceful coexistence for all lengths and for letting women wear whatever they please.'

There were no new Paris sensations from the couturiers for spring 1968. Several designers tried to relaunch the see-through top, especially Yves Saint Laurent. At Courrèges, a model pranced out in Bermuda shorts with two flowers painted on her bared bosom. There was a hint of 1930s revivalism with longer hems for evening, and some models were styled 'a la hippie', with flowing hair. Skirt suits were still being shown in Paris but not as much as before. Paris was picking up on the American look of creatively assembling outfits from a mix of separates and accessories: belts, scarves, skirts, sweaters, blouses, ties, coats, jackets, trousers, sunglasses and jewelry. It was called the 'rich hippie' look by some, but Gloria Vanderbilt called it 'bits-and-pieces' dressing to create a collage of elegance. The previous year Vanderbilt had denounced contemporary fashion as 'grotesque', but by 1968 she had realized the benefits of the new way of dressing, declaring that women had more freedom and choice and that she was spending less on clothes and having more fun.

The exotic East became a strong inspiration with the adoption of the open waistcoat or vest, often in luxurious materials and elegant embroideries. The style quickly became a staple in the repertoire of wardrobe separates. The taste for eastern exoticism extended to pattern-on-pattern fashions and cluttery looks for jewelry, from multiple gold chains to rings on every finger. Belly-dancers' costumes inspired bare midriffs – a sexy contrast to all the sweet ruffled dresses. In its year-end review, *Life* called 1968 the year of the guru: 'Maharishi Mahesh Yogi – Beatles and Mia Farrow' set the fashions. Boutique shopping was no longer for the young. Older women scoured the boutiques that stocked exotic goods from the Middle and Far East in search of interesting scarves, necklaces, embroidered vests and jewelled belts.

For the less bohemian, the shirtwaist dress was popular in the US for evening. Available in mini, midi and maxi lengths, evening shirtwaists debuted in 1968 resort collections and remained popular throughout the year. The waistline was firmly back in 1968: Norman Norell and Yves Saint Laurent had featured wide belts in their autumn 1967 collections, and more designers followed in spring. For evening, jewelled sashes were tied about the waist or fastened with a giant buckle, black velvet belts featured clasps, and pearl and bead belts sported eye-catching tasselled ends. For day, wide stretch belts or leather belts with double-pronged buckles and brass rivet eyelets were popular.

Sleeves were long for autumn 1968, although many evening dresses had very open 'V' necklines. Ensemble dressing remained popular for evening with maxi skirts and wide belts being matched up with sweater or blouse tops and open vests or boleros. Continuing the interest in exoticism that launched in the spring, evening clothes were available in a profusion of rich eastern colours, psychedelic and paisley patterns and gold brocade, especially the new lightweight gold Lurex brocades, accented by heavy gold chains for a Renaissance appeal. Nostalgia remained strong, with the appearance of old-fashioned flowery prints for an Old World peasant charm, often updated in saturated neon colours. The 1930s revival was also still pervasive, featuring wide-leg trousers, and collars and cuffs lavished with fur on jackets and coats.

Paris again showed transparent blouses, but although some women bought them, most failed to muster up enough courage to wear the see-through tops without bras or slips. Otherwise, Paris had nothing new to add to fashion, except sobriety. Black was the colour of 1968, perhaps as a sombre reaction to the student riots of late spring. More couturiers were realizing their profession was shrinking. The fundamental change was in the way French women were now buying their clothes. Like everywhere else, women in France wanted to spend less time and money but still wanted the luxury of designer wear. A made-to-order couture dress could cost US $800 or more in 1968 (about $5,000 today), whereas an equally stylish ready-to-wear garment by the same designer could be had at an eighth of the price. Couture models were still being ordered by Seventh Avenue manufacturers who would then mass produce copies, but far fewer than usual. American department stores were also going directly to the source for ready-to-wear, carrying lines of French designer off-the-rack clothes – something that had never really been available before. The change was difficult for the old guard of designers who had been in the business since the 1930s. Although never an official member of the Paris Haute Couture syndicate, Balenciaga closed his doors at the end of 1968, declaring fashion was over.

Fashion wasn't over, of course – it was changing and expanding, taking in more influences from around the world. Scandinavia became a dominant source of style for home furnishings and textiles in the 1950s when Finnish designers Marimekko and Kaisu Heikkilä began designing clothes. By the 1960s they and other designers were becoming internationally known for their Modernist forms of dress that often blended folkloric patterns and styles. *Life* featured Swedish designers in its 27 September 1968 issue: 'Smashing new

Left: Silver-and-gold metallic organza silk evening gown and coat by RICHARD TAM for SARA FREDERICKS, Palm Beach, spring 1968.

Below: Advertisement for the same dress, from *Vogue*, May 1968.

Sara Fredericks
NEW YORK, BOSTON, PALM BEACH

RICHARD TAM for SARA FREDERICKS

Far left: Moroccan dashiki-inspired silk jersey robe by YVES SAINT LAURENT, Paris, c. 1968.

Left: Indian-style gold lamé brocade evening trouser suit by HOUSE OF BRANELL, New York, c. 1968.

Far left: Moroccan dashiki-inspired silk jersey robe by YVES SAINT LAURENT, Paris, *c.* 1968.

Left: Indian-style gold lamé brocade evening trouser suit by HOUSE OF BRANELL, New York, *c.* 1968.

Opposite left: Detail showing the built-in necklace pendant on the HOUSE OF BRANELL trouser suit (this page), New York, *c.* 1968.

Opposite right: Layered separates, embroidery and jewelry makes a 'rich hippie' look by LANVIN, Paris, autumn 1968.

source of savvy styles…the designs combine an international viewpoint with national traditions. Patterns and colourings often stem from folk sources.' The knit dresses, kaftans, midi coats and jumpsuits featured in the article included designs by Marianne Ohm, Countess von Eckermann, Inez Svensson, Annamodeller, Katja of Sweden, Bertil Wahl, Margareta Westberg (known as 'Tonnie'), Roudi Heintz, Sighsten Herrgård, Gunilla Axén and others. Clothing exports from Scandinavia quadrupled between 1966 and 1969 spurring on the creation of the Scandinavian Fashion Group, an organization of five Swedish and four Danish manufacturer-designers who banded together to show their fashions abroad, including in New York and Tokyo in 1970.

Wherever you looked – Sweden, France or the US – autumn 1968 collections showed more midi and maxi lengths. Maxi

coats from the Paris boutique Micmac were popular imports in New York stores. More buyers slowly moved to longer styles, especially in coats, although some women had the coats shortened to match the length of their mini dresses, about three to five inches above the knee. Although few skirts were dropping very far in length, maxi coats found some favour and skirts did get a little fuller, often A-line and gathered at the waist to create a softer look.

For fashion-conscious older women who felt miniskirts were too young and midi skirts too dowdy, trousers became the solution for many occasions. Trouser suits were sold in profusion during 1968, from work to evening wear, although some facilities still barred women from entry for wearing trousers, even at sporting events like the Henley Regatta, which had banned trouser suits for years. In April 1968, when American fashion designer Betsey Johnson arrived at New York's City Hall to marry John Cale, she was turned away for wearing a burgundy crushed-velvet tunic over a pair of matching trousers. 'I went home and then I came back without the pants…. Definitely showing crotch,' she recalled in a 2003 interview with *New York* magazine.

Ensembles of tunics over matching trousers were successful sellers because it was like getting two outfits for the price of one. Inspired by the traditional Pakistani salwar kameez, Stan Herman of Mr. Mort had created a fashion version for spring 1968 but was told by Mildred Custin of Bonwit Teller that they wouldn't sell because women wouldn't be allowed into restaurants wearing them. A month later, Custin called Herman to tell him that Yves Saint Laurent had done the exact same look and that she would reserve the front windows for Herman's collection.

Above left: YVES SAINT LAURENT, Paris, autumn 1968: black is back.

Above right: JEAN PATOU, Paris, autumn 1968: nostalgia on the rise.

Right: Dress with jewelled appliqué simulating a pocket purse by LANVIN, autumn 1968.

Far right: LANVIN knock-off with jewelled appliqué simulating a necklace c. 1968.

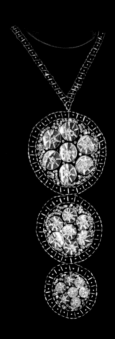

Above: Belted tartan coat by
PIERRE CARDIN, Paris, autumn 1968.

Left: Wide-belted dress by
LOUIS FÉRAUD, Paris, autumn 1968.

Right: Tunic over trousers by NINA RICCI, Paris, autumn 1968.

Middle: Le Smoking suit by YVES SAINT LAURENT, Paris, spring 1967.

Far right: Midi-length trousers by SCHERRER, Paris, autumn 1968.

Most trousers were now quite wide, slightly flared or straight from the hips down, like the slacks worn by Marlene Dietrich in the 1930s. Yves Saint Laurent had a hit with wide, long evening culottes in black velvet for his Rive Gauche boutiques, paired with long-sleeved pullover tops. He was in New York in late September to open his first Rive Gauche boutique in the US. At the opening, women came to greet him wearing trousers; Yves Saint Laurent had gained a reputation for being the inventor of trouser suits, much as Mary Quant had with the miniskirt. Even though he hadn't invented them, he was being credited with their overwhelming presence in fashion, due mostly to his 'Le Smoking' evening suit that remained in production every year after its debut in 1966.

Bolstering the role of trousers in women's wardrobes, Geraldine Stutz, president of Henri Bendel in New York, crusaded for the well-cut trouser suit as the most appropriate choice for city wear. *Life* reported on 18 October 1968 that some restaurants were still in a quandary about whether or not to permit trousers: 'Miss Stutz for one says, "I would rather change my restaurant than my clothes."'

To combat the trend, many companies issued office dress codes – a checklist of secretarial dos and don'ts that said trousers were a 'don't'. In October 1970 *Rags* featured an exposé on American corporate dress during the previous few years, saying that 'since late 1969, one never sees…Pacific Telephone employees with tinted stockings or IBM secretaries with hair longer than shoulder length. Similarly, the First National Bank of New York refuses to so much as interview job applicants who wear pantsuits…. Miss Sullivan, ATT's personnel interviewer, reports that there is no written dress code or policy, however the girls are not allowed to wear pants, culottes, shorts or slacks.'

The Bank of America laid down the dress law in a booklet with a writing style that feigned a newspaper advice column: 'Just let your good taste take over, like choosing fashions that

Right: Silk jersey pyjama trouser suit, by KEN SCOTT, New York, spring 1969.

Far right: Print silk chiffon jumpsuit, worn by Mildred Custin, by JAMES GALANOS, New York, 1968.

Below: Printed velour hostess robe, labelled 'Made in Finland – REVONTULI – SUOMEN TRIKOD', *c.* 1968–70.

are "in" but not way out. To help you avoid mistakes…here are some recommendations…. Save pantsuits, pant dresses, culottes for another scene (yes, including those that do look like skirts).'

Some offices gave in to pressure from female workers. The Columbia Broadcasting System (CBS) headquarters in New York issued a memo on 13 January 1970 stating, 'Please be advised that it is not Company Policy nor the discretion of the immediate supervisor for female employees to wear slacks during the course of their normal working hours.' A week later, fifty women in solidarity wore slacks into the CBS office for a well-publicized revolt against company rules. CBS refused to publicly comment on the protest but never again enforced the 'no slacks' rule. Wishing to avoid similar acts of subversion, the US Attorney's Office sent out a memo on 20 November 1970 allowing female employees to wear trousers as long as

'we can count on your usual good taste, so that visitors will not mistake the office for a Greenwich Village coffee house'.

Trousers, unlike micro miniskirts with hemlines eight or nine inches above the knee, could not be dismissed as inappropriate office attire. However, a statement that reportedly appeared in a dress code booklet for office workers at the textile manufacturer J. P. Stevens stated: 'If you work for a man, you should represent him in a manner that doesn't make him nervous.' Perhaps it was the growing women's liberation movement that was at the root of the trouser ban.

Feminism was gaining momentum in 1968 when a story emerged in September about militant protestors removing their brassieres and burning them in protest of the Miss America Beauty contest in Atlantic City. Although no bras were actually burned, several trappings of femininity were ceremoniously tossed into a 'freedom trash can', including

Far left: Trouser outfit in a window display at Bergdorf Goodman, New York, January 1970.

Left: Chocolate-brown leather trouser suit by CARDINALE, Madrid, *c.* 1969–70.

Opposite left: Trousers and overdress by GEOFFREY BEENE, New York, autumn 1969.

Opposite right: Plaid wool trouser suit, YVES SAINT LAURENT, Paris, autumn 1969.

bras, girdles, cosmetics and high-heeled shoes. The story of the burning bra was the result of a misunderstood metaphor created by a journalist who equated the burning of draft cards in protest of Vietnam to feminists hypothetically burning the bra of oppression.

The body was on display more than ever in spring 1969. Although most dresses had long sleeves, hemlines were higher, barely covering the bottom. The ideal bra-less figure was featured in 'clingers' – languorously fitted dresses in silk jersey, panne velvet, crêpe-back satin and psychedelic-print chiffon. The best clingers were by Pucci in his signature-print lightweight silk jersey. There were plenty of Pucci imitators – Bessi, Leonard, Mr. Dino, Paganne, Maurice – but none managed to copy that lighter-than-air silk jersey from which only Pucci's dresses were made.

Trouser suits, though still not accepted everywhere, were now being treated as serious fashion, rather than a passing oddity. For evening they remained popular, some with legs cut so full they looked like maxi skirts. In keeping with the fuller trousers and skirts, accessories were growing in size – shoes were getting chunkier, with high, wide heels and broad toes, and most purses were now large shoulder-slung satchels.

A mixed bag of inspirations could be seen in younger people's clothes. In its 10 October issue, *Life* reported on the American high-school fashions of autumn 1969 that included a baffling range of styles: Pucci tights, Mexican ponchos, jeans, jumpsuits, shawls, fringed doeskin jackets, Indian headbands: '…wear your own thing. Or someone else's thing – like a print by Pucci, an outfit someone discarded at the Goodwill, or Mom's old lace tablecloth. This freaky new freedom…makes the very idea of school-imposed dress codes seem hopelessly old-fashioned…. Some of the new styles bear prestigious boutique labels, but the most original outfits are the ones fashioned by the girls themselves. They shop at strange places – dime stores, thrift shops – and sew old brocade curtains into flowing coats.'

Nostalgia was also the new young look in Britain and at the head of the revival was Biba, the boutique that best bridged the crossover styles from the 1960s to the 1970s. Polish-born Barbara Hulanicki started Biba as a mail-order fashion business in the early 1960s, creating her biggest seller with a pink gingham dress made available through a reader's offer in the *Daily Mirror*. The profit generated from that design financed the opening of her first boutique in 1964. Cathy McGowan, presenter of the mod music show *Ready Steady Go!*, was a fan of Biba and wherever McGowan shopped, her fans followed. After a couple of smaller locations, an old carpet shop on Kensington High Street was renovated into a Biba mega-boutique in 1969. Following Quant's expansion into cosmetics in 1967, the new boutique also launched a cosmetics line. Biba's clothes were known for their nostalgic mix of Edwardiana and Hollywood glamour, including Art Deco-print dresses in mulberry, rust and plum: 'Dull, sad auntie colours…. They looked better in England's grey light, almost vibrant against the grey buildings and pavements,' recalled Barbara Hulanicki in her autobiography *From A to Biba*.

In a second invasion of British boutique style, Clobber, a London enterprise owned by Jeff Banks and Tony Harley, was contracted to design a line for the American junior label Mindy Malone for autumn 1968. That September the London boutique Annacat opened a New York branch on Madison Avenue, a few blocks north of Paraphernalia, and Biba also expanded into the US, opening a department at Bergdorf Goodman in 1970.

Midi and maxi skirts and coats appeared again for autumn 1969, and this time the maxi coat took off among younger customers who often paired them with either trousers or short skirts. On 7 November *Life* reported disapprovingly that skirts had become so short that they had provoked a counter-revolution: 'No one had expected girls to go to that length of repercussion. Yet here is the street-sweeping hemline, replacing the graceful swing of the mini with a strangled gait, a garment that goes up stairs with the greatest reluctance and sets bystanders guffawing when it tries to get on or off a bus.' In the US, Victor Joris for Cuddlecoat designed some of the best maxi coats – his fur-trimmed, sash-belted designs were worn night or day.

Jumpsuits, in ribbed knits for the young in figure and less clingy materials for everyone else, were popular, as were pyjama trouser suits made up in soft, fluid floral prints, especially by Halston in the US. For daytime, ensemble dressing was still the way, now made more complicated by the necessity of layering clothes artfully for the best effect.

For evening many women chose long-sleeved shirtwaist dresses, both short and long, in silver frosted lace, glittery gold or silver brocade gauze, lined through the body for modesty but transparent through the sleeves. Another popular evening look revived turn-of-the-century glamour with patchwork skirts (a rage for autumn 1969), sheer blouses, ropes of pearls, shoes with curved heels and upswept hairstyles piled atop the head in a puffed chignon borrowed from Edwardian chocolate-box beauties, with tendrils deliberately pulled out around the face.

Attempts to revive longer hemlines had been hampered for years by resistance from younger women reluctant to hide their leggy assets. The first official protest against longer hemlines appeared on 14 March 1968, when the *New York Times* reported on the Mobilization of Militant Miniskirters – a group of young women in their late twenties who had spent their adolescence in petticoats and were against the return of longer, fuller skirts and cinched waists. The group wrote to dress manufacturers and presidents of department stores to convince them that longer hemlines would be a mistake; 'Midis are Monstrous' read one of the protestors' signs.

Seventeen magazine fashion director Rosemary McMurtry admitted in a 1 December 1967 article for *Time*, 'I hope that adult women will stop trying to look like kids, it's a disaster when they do, and develop their own look.' Mrs Loel Guinness lamented in 1968, 'If you dress like a decent person, you are made to feel you are a million years old. If you dress young, you look like an idiot. What choice is there?' The solution was for fashion to break apart into different styles, available simultaneously to different markets with different lifestyles, needs and outlooks. Bill Blass, interviewed by *Life* in June 1969, described the current state of the fashion industry: 'The seasons…don't exist any more. There is only hot and cold,' and age had become a state of mind: 'When the fashion business talks about people over thirty what they really mean is over forty…. Courrèges would have slit his throat if he could have seen some of the ladies in Palm Beach, who must be over seventy, in his dresses. But they say it gives them a new feeling of instant youth. You can never underestimate that feeling of youth. It's what is behind the whole fashion picture – male and female.'

Above: Embroidered shoes designed by MOYA BOWLER for JERRY EDOUARD, *c.* 1969–70.

Left: ROSINA FERRAGAMO shoes, *c.* 1969–70, that pick up on the trend for patchwork.

Far left: Apricot silk dress with full sleeves by LANVIN, Paris, March 1969.

Left: Medieval-style gown by MARILYN BROOKS, Unicorn Boutique, Toronto, 1971.

Opposite: Wool coat and skirt outfit with patent leather trim (left) and a variation of the same style in a vinyl maxi coat (right), both by PIERRE CARDIN, Paris, autumn 1969.

The success of midi and maxi coats during 1969 opened the door to longer skirts. *Women's Wear Daily*, a trade paper that had transformed itself into a popular fashion daily, pretentiously called the midi calf-length hem *longuette* – a word plucked from *Cassell's New French Dictionary* and defined as a feminine and colloquial adjective meaning 'longish'. The French, however, called the style *sous le mollet*, or *le long look*. The paper reported on the *longuette* style nearly every day during early 1970. Manufacturers, worried about a recent slump in the economy combined with rising inflation, didn't want to invest in a style that was not going to sell. Many Seventh Avenue designers called *Women's Wear Daily* 'a sinister influence', among other epithets, for using the power of the daily paper to try to influence public thought. Industry subscribers

registered their discontent by writing letters that the paper printed: 'I think you are doing quite a disservice to manufacturers and retailers by trying to promote a fashion that the customers are not ready for,' said Leon Zwick of Zwick's Ladies Store in Herrin, Illinois. Similarly, 'You are cramming this look down the throats of all women, much against their will,' said G. M. Katz of Universal Shirt Co. in Elizabeth, New Jersey.

The topic was hotly debated in fashion circles. Journalists asked designers, celebrities and anyone with an opinion what they thought about mini and midi skirts. An October 1971 *Rags* article reported that Coco Chanel had never liked minis, saying they were 'indecent…an exhibition of meat'. Valentino was also not a fan, and did not show one miniskirt in his spring 1970 collection: 'I wanted a return to elegance after so many

years of bad taste,' he said. Givenchy also favoured the longer length, as it 'gives a more delicate and languid look'. Georges Pompidou, Richard Nixon and Doris Day also entered the debate in favour of midis. Shorter hem lovers included the outspoken Jacques Tiffeau, who said, 'I will not be pushed around by *Women's Wear Daily*,' and Pauline Trigère, who felt the longer-length clothes were 'unhappy fashions – they're against anything modern'; weighing in on their side were Paul Newman and Rock Hudson.

Most women rejected the midi for its old-fashioned look as protests by fans of miniskirts escalated. The merits of the midi versus the mini were even debated on television by journalist Barbara Walters on the *Today* show. Hollywood was anxious for a resolution to the hemline crisis, as films are usually shot a year in advance of release. Costumers made the most of trouser suits and directors used more shots from the waist up to compensate for the indeterminate hem length. *Life* reported that manufacturers had stocked up to 40 per cent of skirts in midi lengths for spring 1970, and some stores stocked up to 95 per cent of skirts in midi lengths for autumn: the trend was clear. On 3 August 1970, saleswomen at Bonwit's were given the option of wearing either midi skirts or trouser suits. No minis. Martha Needham, the public relations executive at Bonwit's in Chicago, forbade sales personnel from speaking with the press. *Rags* reported on the knee cover-up in October 1970, interviewing staff from the store who would only speak

Above and right: Black-and-white empire-waist dress by GEOFFREY BEENE, New York, spring 1969.

Opposite left: Woman in knitted jumpsuit modelling a macramé necklace from the Museum of Contemporary Art in New York, December 1969.

Opposite right: Protest against midi lengths, Miami, 13 July 1970.

anonymously: 'We were all told to cover our knees and offered a liberal discount on midi stock…. I just brought all my old things in and had my hems dropped. Quite a few of our customers are doing that too.' Ultimately the longer hemlines became successful when they were paired with boots for autumn 1970; the midi was now appealing, and sales improved. Mary Quant, who had asserted the mini was forever, was soon back to making longer skirts, explaining that 'the mini has served its purpose of proving that woman is emancipated…. We can get back to normal.'

Even as hemlines fell, the trend for bareness was not over. Hot pants unexpectedly arrived in resort collections just in time for Christmas 1970. Despite the improbable timing the style met with success. They were as popular in Paris and London as New York and Los Angeles, with versions available from Dorothée Bis, Mary Quant, Mr. Freedom and Giorgio Sant'Angelo. The trend for the bare look continued into 1971 and 1972 with the adoption of halter, tank and tube tops. However, despite the near-nude look of summer 1972, the tattoos of astrological signs and butterfly motifs that were becoming popular with female clients were still not usually visible, at least not until 1973, when the string bikini (a fashion introduced from Brazil) and streaking made headlines.

The home-made look that came in with the hippie movement continued into the early 1970s. Seizing the opportunity to promote indigenous workmanship, in 1970 the US Department of Commerce promoted a two-year-old cooperative of Appalachian quilters and seamstresses in West Virginia who hand-crafted a line of fashions under the label Mountain Artisans.

For thrifty chic the handmade trend extended to adding appliqués, embroidery, studs and patches, hand-painting, and bleaching jeans to customize their appearance, as well as converting jeans into maxi skirts. Sweatshirt and T-shirt art was also on the rise with more examples of home-made, hand-made and boutique-made shirts on the street. The pictures that decorated these varied from fairy-tale and cartoon characters to political heroes, and from nostalgic-inspired Art Deco images to Peter Max-style artscapes.

In July 1970, *Life* featured Jane Forth, the latest new face in the world of modelling, known for her Jean Harlow-style high arched eyebrows. She was pictured in the magazine wearing 1930s and 1940s gowns found for $12.50 each at a Los Angeles vintage clothing store, and worn with a choker – the latest look in jewelry. Nostalgia dressing was no longer just a trend for the young, available at vintage stores or boutiques like Biba where most of the clothes looked like they were made in the 1930s or 1940s. For spring 1971 Busby Berkeley showgirls and Art Deco-era movie queens were the inspiration for Halston's 'movie-star dresses' of slinky bias-cut jersey. Valentino received rave reviews for his collection that same season, based on old Myrna Loy and Rita Hayworth movies.

In Paris, Yves Saint Laurent received a less enthusiastic response for his wartime 1940s-inspired fashions, which brought back unpleasant memories of the occupation years that had divided the country. He hadn't invented the wartime revival look, however; he had borrowed it from Biba and other English boutiques. In 1970 Blair Sabol of the *Village Voice* accused: 'Saint Laurent has been ripping off the kids' gear for years,' but he had always managed to bring French chic to whatever he borrowed – until now. He veered too close to vulgar, and the press mercilessly skewered his collection, perhaps most viciously in a review by fashion critic Eugenia Sheppard that resulted in her being banned from Yves Saint Laurent fashion shows for several years. Despite negative reviews for his spring 1971 collection, Saint Laurent not only survived, he learned from his mistakes and stayed in touch with his clientele, going on to become the most important Paris designer of the 1970s. In the summer of 1971 he announced he would be abandoning haute couture. At the same time he expanded his business to include men's ready-to-wear as well as a men's

Right: Boots anchor the midi: CHRISTIAN DIOR, Paris, autumn 1969.

Far right: Midi coats over trousers by DONALD BROOKS, New York, autumn 1969.

fragrance: Pour Homme. The advertisement featured a nude photograph of Saint Laurent posed on a leather cushion.

Life reported in October 1971 that Saint Laurent had gone through a crisis in 1966 when he saw the younger generation shaking off the old taboos in clothes, outlook and behaviour. 'I just could no longer take part in the fashion circus… I saw it all as fake. And with every passing season it got worse,' he admitted. His evening trouser suit 'Le Smoking' was a favourite with fashion editors in 1966 and was featured in every major fashion publication, but he did not sell one couture model of the tuxedo suit. It was only after he created a boutique version that sales were brisk for this famous outfit. It was then that he realized how much fashion had changed and understood that it could come from anywhere; daily life was where clothes designers

belonged and they had to keep their eyes open. 'The challenge with ready-to-wear is to make something which looks just as good on a girl of fifteen as a woman of sixty,' he explained.

Many trends and styles that had started during or gained momentum in the 1960s went on to define the 1970s and beyond. *Women's Wear Daily* noted in July 1968, 'The Kooks, the Kids, and the Hippies got people to start thinking in a fresh way. You may not agree with them, but you can't ignore them. They freed themselves…and gave others the courage to do the same.' A quiet revolution had taken place but it was as dramatic a change as there had ever been in the history of dress. There were still rules of dressing for success if you wished to rise through the old establishment of business or society, but most rules for most occasions were being toppled. 'Nowadays

Above: Suede knickers and
midi skirt shown with boots,
Bergdorf Goodman, New York,
November 1970.

Right: Leather and suede outfit
with midi hemline but mini slit
in front, *c.* 1970.

the doorman doesn't know who to let in,' commented Marshall McLuhan in an October 1970 *Rags* interview. Style had taken the place of fashion, and style could come from anywhere and be worn by anyone. The very delineators of *la mode*, fashion magazines, were losing advertisers in droves. In July 1971 *Vogue* attempted to reinvigorate its failing circulation by installing Grace Mirabella as editor-in-chief, replacing Diana Vreeland, who had seen the transformation of fashion since joining the magazine in 1962.

The biggest fashion story of the 1970s that had its roots in the 1960s was the denim takeover. Jeans had humble origins and a working-class history, but they rose to become a status symbol of rebellion and standard garb of the world's youth. Many businesses targeted blue jeans as inappropriate office wear – even the head office of Levi's in San Francisco,

although it would be one of the first companies to repeal its no-jeans policy in autumn 1970. For most offices, a no-denim rule remained in place until 'casual Fridays' broke down the last vestiges of office attire in the 1990s. At the dawn of the 1970s, jeans were being worn as cut-offs on the beaches of St Tropez and on the streets of every style-conscious city. Bales of tattered American jeans were exported to France where they were re-cut, and there was a thriving underground blue-jean market in the Soviet Union. Sweden only began to allow the import of American jeans in 1970, but by 1972 American production couldn't keep up with world demand. The most important international fashion of the twentieth century had become ubiquitous. Without the strict observance of fashion, the inherent rules of dressing for occasion were diminished, and a new kind of conformity set in.

Far left: Hot pants in Macy's department store window, New York, January 1971.

Left: The knee-high boot, introduced in the late 1960s, became the most popular style of the early 1970s; it could be worn with miniskirts, hot pants, midi and maxi skirts, as well as knickers and trousers.

Above left: Maxi sweater dress by PIERRE CARDIN, Paris, autumn 1969.

Above right: Purple cotton corduroy maxi-coat by BIBA, London, c. 1968–69.

Right: Transparent blouse by OSCAR DE LA RENTA, Paris, and unlabelled gypsy skirt, c. 1969–70.

References

Books

Akhtar, Mariam, and Steve Humphries, *The Fifties and Sixties: A Lifestyle Revolution* (London, 2001)

Bender, Marylin, *The Beautiful People* (New York, 1967)

Bernard, Barbara, *Fashion in the Sixties* (London, 1978)

Bleikorn, Samantha, *Mini Mod Sixties Book* (San Francisco, 2002)

Braunstein, Peter, and Michael William Doyle, *Imagine Nation: The American Counterculture of the 1960s and 70s* (New York, 2002)

Bultitude, Millicent, *Get Dressed: A Useful Guide to London's Boutiques* (London, 1966)

Cawthorne, Nigel, *Key Moments in Fashion* (London, 1998)

Etchingham, Kathy, *Through Gypsy Eyes: My Life, The 60s, and Jimi Hendrix* (London, 1999)

Fogg, Marnie, *Boutique: A 60s Cultural Phenomenon* (London, 2003)

Halliday, Leonard, *The Fashion Makers* (London, 1966)

Hill, Daniel Dellis, *American Menswear* (Lubbock, 2011)

Hulanicki, Barbara, *From A to Biba: The Autobiography of Barbara Hulanicki* (London, 2007)

Lester, Richard, *Boutique London* (Suffolk, 2010)

Lester, Richard, *John Bates: Fashion Designer* (Bath, 2008)

Lester, Richard, *Photographing Fashion British Style in the Sixties* (Bath, 2009)

Lobenthal, Joel, *Radical Rags: Fashions of the Sixties* (New York, 1990)

Lynman, Ruth, *Couture: An Illustrated History of the Great Paris Designers and Their Creations* (New York, 1972)

Marwick, Arthur, *The Sixties* (Oxford, 1998)

Milbank, Carolyn, *New York Fashion* (New York, 1989)

Miles, Barry, *Hippie* (New York, 2003)

Morris, Bernadine, *The Fashion Makers* (New York, 1978)

Morris, Brian, and Ernestine Carter, *An Introduction to Mary Quant's London* [exhibition catalogue] (London, 1973)

Pitti Foundation, *Italian Eyes* (Milan, 2005)

Polhemus, Ted, *Street Style* (London, 1994)

Quant, Mary, *Quant by Quant* (Bath, 1966; New York, 1967)

Reed, Jeremy, *The King of Carnaby Street: The Life of John Stephen* (London, 2010)

Ross, Geoffrey Aguilina, *The Day of the Peacock Style for Men 1963–1973* (London, 2011)

Sandbrook, Dominic, *White Heat: A History of Britain in the Swinging Sixties* (London, 2006)

Shrimpton, Jean, *An Autobiography* (London, 1990)

Steele, Valerie, *Fashion, Italian Style* (New York, 2003)

Stegemeyer, Anne, *Who's Who in Fashion, Third Edition* (New York, 1996)

Strodder, Chris, *Swingin' Chicks of the Sixties* (New York, 2000)

Articles

1960

'High Style at Low Cost', *Life*, 14 March 1960

'Odds on Bet: Next Woman You See Will Wear These', *Life*, 28 March 1960

'Five Beauties Steal the Paris Shows', *Life*, 12 September 1960

'Norell', *Life*, 26 September 1960

'Seventh Rules Nation's Style' (New York clothing industry), *Life*, 3 October 1960

'Perils of Spike Heels', *Life*, 10 October 1960

'British Couple Kooky Styles', *Life*, 5 December 1960

1961

'The St. Tropez Way for the U.S.A.', *Life*, 13 January 1961

'You Don't Have to Look Hard to See Another Jackie', *Life*, 20 January 1961

'Sensible Shoes Step Out in Style', *Life*, 24 March 1961

'Pants by Any Other Name', *New York Times*, 21 April 1961

'Fashion Designer Hires Negro Model', *New York Times*, 23 June 1961

'Hip Hung Pants', *Life*, 25 August 1961

'Beards are Back', *Life*, 8 September 1961

'Entering with a Flourish – The Age of the Hairdresser', *Life*, 3 November 1961

'Italian Fashions', *Life*, 1 December 1961

1962

'Cleopatra is Back Men', *Life*, 2 February 1962

'Pay Your Money Take Your Copy', *Life*, 6 April 1962

'Prints Take a Dizzy Turn', *Life*, 13 April 1962

'The Wig is With Us', *Life*, 18 May 1962

'By Any Name – Still a Sack', *Life*, 15 June 1962

'Now the Marienbad Cut's In', *Life*, 22 June 1962

'Negro Models – a Band of Beautiful Pioneers', *Life*, 29 June 1962

'English Countries Stress Simpler Cut and Design', *New York Times*, 23 July 1962

'Around the World Jet Shopper', *Life*, 3 August 1962

'Boys and Girls Too Old Too Soon', *Life*, 10 August 1962

'New St. Tropez Style', *Life*, 24 August 1962

'First Color Views of '62 Paris Styles', *Life*, 31 August 1962

'Bargains from Britain', *Life*, 12 October 1962

'Stars, Styles and Sunshine' (California fashion), *Life*, 19 October 1962

'Poor Little Rich Furs', *Life*, 2 November 1962

1963

'A Princess Sets a Style' (Princess Galitzene), *Life*, 1 February 1963

'A Barefoot Tycoon Makes Lillies Bloom All Over' (Lilly Pulitzer), *Life*, 8 February 1963

'Norell and Galanos', *Life*, 1 March 1963

'Good Grief! Garbo? – Garbo Style', *Life*, 5 April 1963

'Bygone Beauty is Back – New Fashions Go Romantic', *Life*, 17 May 1963

'Teenagers Agree on Fashions They Like', *Life*, 3 July 1963

'Fall Fashions from New York', *Life*, 12 July 1963

'Mad New Dazzle is Coming to the Campus', *Life*, 16 August 1963

'Elegant At-Ease Look – New Paris fashions', *Life*, 30 August 1963

'A Young Designer Changes Things – Slava Zaitsev', *Life*, 13 September 1963

'Sporty Jumpers are Made in Plaid', *New York Times*, 19 September 1963

'Rudi Gernreich, Recipient of American Fashion Critics' Award', *Life*, 4 October 1963

'Brash New Breed of British Designers', *Life*, 18 October 1963

1964

'Necklines Take the Plunge', *Life*, 3 January 1964

'Here Come Those Beatles', *Life*, 31 January 1964

'Everywhereness of the Chanel Look (The)', *Life*, 14 February 1964

'Lure of Lacy Legs', *Life*, 28 February 1964

'Les Locomotive – The Young Socialites of Paris Fashion', *Life*, 6 March 1964

'Emmanuelle Khanh', *Life*, 13 March 1964

'Mail-Order Chic – Sears Stems the Bareheaded Time with Big Names', *Life*, 20 March 1964

The Mod's Monthly, April 1964

'A New Kind of Sweater Girl', *Life*, 10 April 1964

The Mod's Monthly, May 1964

'Hooray for the YéYé Girls', *Life*, 29 May 1964

'Young Designers Set Pace in Britain: Vital New Fashions Win Following in Europe and U.S.', *New York Times*, 3 June 1964

'Pajamas Put On Party Airs', *Life*, 5 June 1964

'Topless Cocktail Gowns Being Sold in London', *New York Times*, 22 June 1964

'And Not a Stitch on Underneath', *Life*, 3 July 1964

'Me? In That! – The Topless Bathing Suit', *Life*, 10 July 1964

'Stylist Gets Cue from Far East', *New York Times*, 22 July 1964

'Long Hem Is High Light of Mary Quant Pattern', *New York Times*, 27 July 1964

'Fall Elegance – American Evening Styles', *Life*, 28 August 1964

'So Young, Elegant Juvenile Look of Paris Fall Fashions', *Life*, 4 September 1964

'The Young in Revolt – Japanese Youth Run Away from Tradition', *Life*, 11 September 1964

'Dazzling Flair from Spain' *Life*, 9 October 1964

'A Nobel Nose to the Grindstone – Pucci', *Life*, 16 October 1964

'Pants for the City?', *Life*, 23 October 1964

'Accent on Youth', *New York Times*, 25 October 1964

'Captivating Comeback for Crochet', *Life*, 30 October 1964

'Op Art', *Life*, 11 December 1964

'A Pretty Parisian Profusion of Pants', *Life*, 11 December 1964

1965

'Style Trends Were Started By the Young', *New York Times*, 1 January 1965

'Fashion for the Beach', *Life*, 8 January 1965

'Women's Wear Maker Bemoans Declining Sales in His Industry', *New York Times*, 22 February 1965

'Styles Too Are Pushed Further Out by Pop', *Life*, 26 February 1965

'Molyneux Makes Comeback with First Paris Collection in 15 Years', *Life*, 5 March 1965

'Underground Clothes', *Life*, 19 March 1965

'Dissent Voiced on Paris Designs', *New York Times*, 19 March 1965

'One Shouldered Dresses', *Life*, 25 March 1965

'The Sleek Space Flair in Plastics', *Life*, 9 April 1965

'It's OP from Toe to Top', *Life*, 16 April 1965

'Arbiter of the Taste of France – Editor Madame Lazareff of Elle', *Life*, 30 April 1965

'So Now I Own a Net Bikini', *Life*, 7 May 1965

'More Girl Than Sweater', *Life*, 14 May 1965

'The Lord of the Space Ladies – Courrèges', *Life*, 21 May 1965

'The Sugar and Spice Look', *Life*, 28 May 1965

'A Politely Dark View of Things – Sunglasses', *Life*, 4 June 1965

'Abracadabra, it's a Grand New Hat Trick – Scarf Hats by Halston', *Life*, 18 June 1965

'Getting into Jams at the Beach', *Life*, 25 June 1965

'Coty Jury Votes Special Citations but No Winnie', *New York Times*, 30 June 1965

'Sassoon and His Scissors', *Life*, 9 July 1965

'Big Sprout-Out of Male Mop-Tops', *Life*, 30 July 1965

'Paris Couture Is Not as Haut As It Used to Be', *New York Times*, 1 August 1965 'Big Boom in Men's Beauty Aids', *Life*, 13 August 1965

'It's All Got to Match – Dresses with Matching Hats and Spats or Socks', *Life*, 20 August 1965

'A New Move to the Middle Ground From High Fashion and High Prices', *New York Times*, 1 September 1965

'Models Go-Go and so do Fashions', *New York Times*, 2 September 1965

'Fireworks and Feathers – New Paris Styles', *Life*, 3 September 1965

'After Courrèges, What Future for the Haute Couture?', *New York Times*, 12 September 1965

'British and Dizzier Than Ever', *Life*, 17 September 1965

'The Fall Isn't All Knee', *Life*, 1 October 1965

'News of Fashion: New Yves St. Laurent Boutique', *New York Times*, 7 October 1965

'He Shows You the Girl – Jack Hanson and JAX', *Life*, 8 October 1965

'Luminescent Finery', *Life*, 15 October 1965

'Bravura Year for Italian Beauty', *Life*, 22 October 1965

'Here's Art in Your Eye', *Life*, 29 October 1965

'U.S. and Britain Contribute to Frenchmen's New Look', *New York Times*, 29 October 1965

'Designer Decries Men's Styles', *New York Times*, 2 November 1965

'International Necklines – Strapless for Evening', *Life*, 12 November 1965

'The Girl with the Black Tights – Edie Sedgwick', *Life*, 26 November 1965

'The Wild Hue Yonder – Pucci Dresses Airline Stewardesses for the Jet Age', *Life*, 3 December 1965

'Miss Bardot: Just an Old-Fashioned Girl Girl', *New York Times*, 18 December 1965

'Garment Men Emphasize Unity: Trade Associations to Merge', *New York Times*, 27 December 1965

'Fashion Had its Go-go Fling During 1965', *New York Times*, 31 December 1965

1966

'Fashion Industry Holds Its Deadlines', *New York Times*, 6 January 1966

'Dazzle of '66 Prints', *Life*, 14 January 1966

'See-through Vinyl for a Rainy Day', *Life*, 21 January 1966

'Specs to Be Seen In, Not Through', *Life*, 4 February 1966

'Hartnell on Mods', *New York Times*, 1 March 1966

'Nearly Nude Fashions from Paris' (Yves Saint Laurent), *Life*, 4 March 1966

'America Cottons to Lise Lotte – Danish Model Turned Designer', *Life*, 1 April 1966

'Jablow and Pruzan: A Chapter Closes', *New York Times*, 8 April 1966

'And Thereby Hangs the Tale of the Fashionable 4-Inch Necktie', *New York Times*, 9 April 1966

'Mod, Paris', *New York Times*, 17 April 1966

'How Much Higher Will They Go? British Girls in their Showy Thigh-high Skirts', *Life*, 22 April 1966

'Paper Jewelry and Chuck-Away Dresses', *Life*, 29 April 1966

'Revolution in Men's Clothes', *Life*, 13 May 1966

'Legs Are Decked Out', *Life*, 20 May 1966

'Short, Short, Short Skirt Story', *New York Times*, 20 May 1966

'Flashy Bedlam of the Discotheque', *Life*, 27 May 1966

'London Is I'Cumen In, Sing Cu-Cu', *Observer*, 29 May 1966 (reprinted in the *New York Times*)

'Rise of the Fall', *Life*, 3 June 1966

'Fashions to Buy, Wear, Throw Away Gain Favor', *Globe and Mail*, 9 June 1966

'Eye-catching Op for a Swim', *Life*, 10 June 1966

'It's the Fashion Uniform, Granny', *New York Times*, 10 June 1966

'Futuristic Costume? Paper Dresses In', *Seattle Post Intelligencer*, 14 June 1966

'Do-it-Yourself Dress', *New York Times*, 16 June 1966

'Bright Spirit of Marimekko', *Life*, 24 June 1966

'Knee is Fancy Free and Fashionable', *New York Times*, 24 June 1966

'Mary Quant Decides to "Cool It a Bit" in New Line', *New York Times*, 29 June 1966

'Youthful Caprice for Caps', *Life*, 15 July 1966

'Rudi Gernreich's Animal Act' (animal prints), *Life*, 22 July 1966

'Dress for Non-Seamstresses: Glue-it-Yourself', *Life*, 29 July 1966

'Flowing Arabian Splendor in Fall Designs', *Life*, 19 August 1966

'LSD Art – Psychedelia', *Life*, 9 September 1966

'Union Jack Waves in London', *New York Times*, 13 September 1966

'The Cut-Up Kanga Caper', *Life*, 16 September 1966

'She Was Only a Paper Doll', *Financial Post*, 17 September 1966

'Eyes Right for Military Flair', *New York Times*, 30 September 1966

'Pantsuits – Now They've Got it All', *Life*, 7 October 1966

'Bright and Bold Stripes for Fall', *Life*, 14 October 1966

'Fine Feathered Autumn – Feathered Evening Dresses', *Life*, 28 October 1966

'The Wastebasket Dress Has Arrived – Paper Fashions', *Life*, 25 November 1966

'Now Hear This – In London, Old Clothes Are the Latest Noise', *Life*, 2 December 1966

'Canned Dressing – Dresses Sold in Cans by Wippette', *Life*, 9 December 1966

1967

'Jacques Heim, 67, Couturier, Dead', *New York Times*, 9 January 1967

'Public Tries on Paper-Clothing Fad for Size', *New York Times*, 22 January 1967

'Breathe In: The Belt Comes Back', *Life*, 17 February 1967

'Paper Clothing: Fad or Fashion?', *Globe and Mail*, 21 February 1967 (quoting material from *New York Times*)

'Galanos Runs a Good Gamut – Spring Collections', *Life*, 10 March 1967

'Real Live Paper Dolls', *Time*, 17 March 1967

'Buyers Latch onto the Twiggy Boom', *New York Times*, 29 March 1967

'The Princess and the Paper Lash – Coloured Paper Eyelashes', *Life*, 31 March 1967

'Peacock Feathers', *Observer*, 9 April 1967

'Twiggy Makes U.S. Styles Swing Too', *Life*, 14 April 1967

'In Paris, It's Get Rich but Look Poor', 19 April 1967

'Watches to Watch – Oversized Dials with Colorful Bands', *Life*, 21 April 1967

'Looking for Laughs – Sunglasses', *Life*, 16 June 1967

'Paper Dollies Pay for Fun', *Seattle Post-Intelligencer*, 25 May 1967

'Steel for Style – Paco Rabanne', *Life*, 26 May 1967

'The Hippies: Philosophy of a Subculture', *Time*, 7 July 1967

'The Short-cut Pantsuit', *Life*, 23 June 1967

'The Paper Shoe', *Harper's Bazaar*, July 1967

'Shoes With Labels of French Couture', *New York Times*, 21 July 1967

'Cardin's Collection has Familiar Look', *New York Times*, 29 July 1967

'Be a Paper Doll', *Hair-Do*, August 1967

'Under 21 Way-Out Fashion', *Life*, 4 August 1967

'Norell and Galanos Agree that Waistlines and Knees Are In', *New York Times*, 9 August 1967

'Now the Mini has a Man in It', *Life*, 11 August 1967

'Miss Dior Shop a Hit in Paris', *New York Times*, 19 September 1967

'Black Is Back and Worn All Over', *Life*, 20 October 1967

'Leg Art', *Life*, 10 November 1967

'Aboard the Michelangelo, Gowns Were Paper but Chic', *New York Times*, 16 November 1967

'Hemlines – Up, Up & Away', *Time*, 1 December 1967

'The Paper Caper', *Saturday Evening Post*, 2 December 1967

'Klara Rotschild – Hungary's Top Couturier', *Life*, 8 December 1967

'Ruffles, Frills, Lace and Bows', *Life*, 15 December 1967

1968
'Bonnie's Stylish Bang', *Life*, 12 January 1968

'Alas! The Poor Mini', *New York Times*, 4 February 1968

'The Year of the Guru', *Life*, 9 February 1968

'Eeny, Mini, Midi, Maxi', *Life*, 16 February 1968

'Petticoats are Back for Full-Skirted Styles', *Life*, 23 February 1968

'Bonnie Cashin's Paper-Route to Fashion', *American Fabrics*, Spring 1968

'There Were No Sensations from the Paris Spring Collections', *Life*, 1 March 1968

'Poster Dresses Make a Hit', *Winnipeg Free Press*, 3 March 1968

'Mobilization of the Militant Miniskirters', *New York Times*, 14 March 1968

'Now, Mary Defends Her Mini,' *St Petersburg Times*, 26 March 1968

'Put-On Posters', *Life*, 5 April 1968

'67's Twig Becomes a Tree', *Life*, 19 April 1968

'Bolder Lip and Nail Colours, Fuzzy "Hippy" Hairdos', *Life*, 31 May 1968

'Uniworld – Nehru jackets, printed jeans, vests and blouses', *Life*, 21 June 1968

'$15 Kits Based on Paco Rabanne Chain Mail Dresses', *Life*, 7 June 1968

'Stars and Stripes Forever, but Not on a Shirt for Sale', *New York Times*, 11 July 1968

'A Shaggy Goat Story from Afghanistan', *Life*, 26 July 1968

'Clobber Look Moves in on U.S.', *New York Times*, 3 August 1968

'Paris Fashions', *Life*, 30 August 1968

'The Name Is the Game', *Life*, 13 September 1968

'Sweden – A Smashing New Source of Savvy Styles', *Life*, 27 September 1968

'Gloria's Bits and Pieces Add Up to a Lot of Style', *Life*, 4 October 1968

'Wall Street Discovers that There's Gold on Seventh Avenue', *New York Times*, 14 October 1968

'See Through Break Through?', *Life*, 18 October 1968

'Instant Originals', *Time*, 25 October 1968

'Diahann Carroll… Wears Wigs', *Life*, 8 November 1968

'Thirties Glamor Sails Again', *Life*, 22 November 1968

'Renaissance – The Mirrored Alchemy of Gold and Black in a Fashion', *Life*, 6 December 1968

'Jacques Kaplan's Tour de Furs', *Life*, 13 December 1968

1969
'The Incredible Year: '68 Special Issue', *Life*, 10 January 1969

'In Paris It's New Flair and Blue Hair', *Life*, 28 February 1969

'Fantasy Fashions – Sant'Angelo', *Life*, 7 March 1969

'Dior Facing Facts', *New York Times*, 11 April 1969

'Spring Fashions Off to the Races', *Life*, 18 April 1969

'End of a Salon', *New York Times*, 13 May 1969

'Bill Blass – The Man Who Made the Scarsdale Mafia Suit', *Life*, 13 June 1969

'Woodstock Special Edition', *Life*, August 1969

'That New York Look', *Life*, 22 August 1969

'Happy Protest in High School Fashion', *Life*, 10 October 1969

'Maxi to Cardin C'est Bon', *New York Times*, 14 October 1969

'Black Model Breakthrough', *Life*, 17 October 1969

'Maxi Cover-Up', *Life*, 7 November 1969

'Rub-a-dub-dub', *Life*, 12 December 1969

'Men's Fashions in the 1960s: The Peacock's Glory Was Regained', *New York Times*, 15 December 1969

1970
'Fashion for the 1970s – Rudi Gernreich Makes Some Modest Proposals', *Life*, 9 January 1970

'Origin of the Longuette or, as They Say in Paris, "Le Long Look"', *New York Times*, 26 February 1970

'Ad-Lib Fashion Show', *Life*, 27 February 1970

'The Scandinavians Are Lighthearted When it Comes to Designing Clothes', *New York Times*, 9 March 1970

'Onward and Downward with Hemlines', *Life*, 13 March 1970

'Wigs for Men', *Life*, 20 March 1970

'Quota Proposals Dismay Importers', *New York Times*, 15 April 1970

'Even for Its Inventor, Miniskirt Is Dead', *New York Times*, 23 April 1970

'Betsey Johnson', *Rags*, June 1970

'T-Shirt Fashion', *Rags*, June 1970

'Just Plain Jane', *Life*, 4 July 1970

Special issue on hippies, *Time*, 7 July 1967

'Clothes that Tell a Story', *Life*, 17 July 1970

'Homespun High Fashion', *Life*, 31 July 1970

'Neck Deep in Dog Collars', *Life*, 18 September 1970

'Creator of Mini Says Wear What Feels Right', *The Robesonian*, 20 September 1970

'Male Plumage', *Life*, 25 September 1970

'Mini Skirt Tribalism – Fashion Fascism – An Interview with Marshall McLuhan', *Rags*, October 1970

'Office Dress Codes', *Rags*, October 1970

'The Midi that Wouldn't Die', *Life*, 30 October 1970

'Stud & Patch & Paint & Bleach' (Jean Art), *Rags*, November 1970

'It's Knickers Sans Droop', *Life*, 27 November 1970

'Office Memorandum Officially Sanctions Pants Suits for Work', *New York Times*, 30 November 1970

'She Was Beautiful' (Janis Joplin), *Rags*, December 1970

1971
'Vintage Clothing', *Rags*, January 1971

'Boutiques and Hip Capitalism', *Rags*, February 1971

'Hot Pants – An Improbable Fashion Fad Arrives Midwinter', *Life*, 29 January 1971

'The Politics of Midi', *Rags*, October 1971

'Yves St. Laurent – Parting Shots: New King of Off the Rack Fashion', *Life*, 8 October 1971

1972
'Couture Alive, Pulse Fading', *New York Times*, 28 January 1972

'Skin Game – The Ancient Art of Tattooing Comes Back into Fashion', *Life*, 10 March 1972

'The Bare Look', *Life*, 28 July 1972

'The World Is Blue-Jean Country Now', *Life*, 24 November 1972

Other articles
'Women's World Abroad: Sleek and Alluring Dynasty Salon', *New York Times*, 8 September 1959

'Remember Those Topless Suits? Rudi Gernreich Returns to the Fashion Swim', *People*, 25 May 1981

'The House of Mod', *New York* magazine, spring 2003

Many issues of *Vogue*, *Harper's Bazaar*, *L'Officiel*, *Elle*, *Seventeen*, *Gentlemen's Quarterly* and other 1960s fashion magazines and newspapers were also consulted.

Films
Blow-Up (1966): A London fashion photographer unwittingly witnesses a murder

Bonnie and Clyde (1967): A retelling of the famous 1930s outlaws

Breakfast at Tiffany's (1961): A New York party girl falls in love with a her gigolo neighbour

Cleopatra (1963): The life of history's most famous Egyptian queen

Doctor Zhivago (1965): A Russian doctor falls in love with a political activist's wife during the Bolshevik Revolution

La Dolce Vita (1960): A series of stories following a week in the life of a Roman paparazzi journalist

Last Year at Marienbad (1961):
French art film about a couple who
may have met before
Smashing Time (1967): Sensible Brenda
and flamboyant Yvonne arrive in
London to seek fame and fortune,
but nothing goes as planned
The World of Suzie Wong (1960):
An artist moves to Hong Kong and
falls in love with a local prostitute
Tom Jones (1963): The randy tales of a
charming British lover
Who Are You, Polly Magoo? (1966):
A satire of the fashion industry
following a fashion model as she
is pursued by a documentary film crew

Index

Page numbers in *italic* refer
to illustrations.

Credits

Garments and accessories illustrated in this book are from the following collections: **Audrey Faye Norman**: Stars and Stripes hip huggers on p. 145; **Brooklyn Museum**: paper dress painted by Andy Warhol on p. 116; **Dugald Costume Museum** (Costume Museum of Canada), Winnipeg, Manitoba: Paco Rabanne dresses on pp. 96–97; **North Vancouver Museum and Archives**: Op art print shoes on p. 82; **Seneca Fashion Resource Centre**, Don Mills, Ontario: green silk quilted coat on p. 11, three black leather shoes on p. 23, Christian Dior striped suit on p. 70, Jean Pierce Op Art coat on p. 89, Claire Haddad lace and chiffon pantsuit on p. 98, embroidered suede dress on p. 143, Cardin green wool dress on p. 177, rhinestone-jeweled black velvet dress on p. 186; Finnish velour robe on p. 189. All other garments and accessories are from the collection of the **Fashion History Museum**, Cambridge, Ontario, Canada.

The lyrics for 'I Was Lord Kitchener's Valet', Words and Music by Phil Coulter and Bill Martin ©, were reproduced by permission of Keith Prowse Music Publishing Co. Ltd, London W8 5SW (pages 128–29).

Lyric from 'Laugh at Me' by Sonny Bono, originally released on Atco Records, 1965 (page 131).

Images appear courtesy of:
Associated Press: p. 132, left.
Corbis Images: p. 8; p. 135; p. 145, right. All © Bettmann/CORBIS.
Dugald Costume Museum (Costume Museum of Canada): pp. 96–97, all.
Getty Images: pp. 52–53, left; p. 54; p. 63, left; p. 75; p. 109; p. 127; p. 132, right; p. 137, right; p. 140, left; p. 159; p. 171.
Horst P. Horst for *Look* magazine, Library of Congress: p. 119, right.
International Wool Fashion Office, Paris, from the archives of the Fashion History Museum, Cambridge, Ontario: p. 61, middle and right; p. 83; p. 88; p. 89, left; p. 93; p. 99; p. 101, left; p. 102; p. 103, left and bottom; p. 105, right; p. 106, left and middle; p. 106, left; p. 107; p. 169; p. 175; p. 176; p. 177, left; p. 178, bottom left; p. 179; p. 180; p. 181, right; p. 185, right; p. 186, left, middle and bottom left; p. 187; p. 188; p. 191, right; p. 195, left; p. 199, left.
Michael Ochs Archives/Getty Images: p. 130; p. 133, right; p. 139, top right.
Popperfoto/Getty Images: p. 33.
Robert Altman: p. 138.
Time Life Pictures/Getty Images: p. 172.
William Klein for US *Vogue*: p. 11, left.
Woolmark Archive, Australian Wool Innovation Limited and the London College of Fashion: p. 60; p. 80, right.

All other images are by the author or are from the library and archives of the **Fashion History Museum**, Cambridge, Ontario, Canada.

Acknowledgments

I would like to thank the following for their help with supplying images, research, and help in creating this book: Kenn Norman, Mike Wilhem, Daniel Milford-Cottam, Lynne K. Ranieri, University for the Creative Arts in Surrey UK, Jody Steinman, Sarah Norris, and the staff at Thames & Hudson for their patience and guidance, especially Jennie Condell and Myfanwy Vernon-Hunt, as well as Jamie Camplin for his flexible deadlines.